# *Weighed by the Word*

## PAT WARREN

REGULAR BAPTIST
RBP **Press**

## DEDICATION

To all the women who built into my life: my grandmother, my mother, my sister, my two daughters and two daughters-in-law, as well as ladies who thought through these particular lessons with me. God used a host of friends, pastors, and, most notably, my husband, to build into my life. To God be the glory!

## ACKNOWLEDGMENTS

Quotation on page 11 is from "What Makes a Body Somebody?" by Dr. Greg Couser. Quote first appeared in the Spring/Summer 2007 issue of *Torch*, published by Cedarville University. Used by permission.

Quotations on page 24 are from *Becoming the Noble Woman* by Anita Young. ©1988 by Hensley Publishing. All rights reserved. Used by permission.

Quotation on page 29 is from *Trusting God: Even When Life Hurts* by Jerry Bridges. ©1990, NavPress Publishing Group. Used by permission of NavPress. All rights reserved. www.navpress.com.

Quotation on page 38 is from *BeAttitudes for Women: Wisdom from Heaven for Life on Earth* by Dorothy Kelley Patterson. ©2008, Wipf & Stock Publishers. Used by permission.

Quotations on page 53 are from "Thank God for Aging" by Charles Dolph. Quote first appeared in the Spring/Summer 2007 issue of TORCH, published by Cedarville University. Used by permission.

Quotations on pages 79 and 80 are from *The Discipline of Grace: God's Role and Our Role in the Pursuit of Holiness* by Jerry Bridges. ©2006, NavPress Publishing Group. Used by permission of NavPress. All rights reserved. www.navpress.com.

# Contents

# Preface

With so much pressure to be body conscious, to watch our diets, to check our weight, to exercise regularly, we continue to measure our bodies by pictures in magazines, ideal weight charts, size of clothes, or numbers on the measuring tape or scale. But in our attempts to "measure up," we often find ourselves discouraged or dissatisfied with ourselves, especially with our bodies. We constantly measure ourselves by numerous *external* standards, and often forget to measure our bodies by the *eternal* standard of the Bible. It is as though we cannot come to terms with our physical bodies.

As Christians, we emphasize our doctrine, our thinking, our minds— all of this being necessary—but we do not quite know how to relate Christianity to the bodies we have to put up with on a day-to-day basis, whether sick, healthy, fat, skinny, etc. One Christian psychologist suggests that we Christians often "live from the neck up." The physical body is an enigma to us.

This dilemma does not come by accident. Satan is out to get us through our bodies! Think of billboards, TV programs, magazines: Satan targets our bodies every way he can. He incites men and the media to exploit the female body. Often, while he's exploiting the body on one hand, Satan, as "an angel of light," cleverly suggests "remedies" for the problems sin causes, remedies that further entangle women and rob them of peace. He steers women farther away from God and His Word.

What does God think? God has an investment in our bodies. He created them; He wants to use them. He has planned a future for them; He will raise them. He sent His Son to inhabit a physical body and to die in a physical body. The Father then raised that physical body so He might redeem our physical bodies. And God the Holy Spirit is content to dwell in the bodies of all who receive the Son. Someday we shall see Christ in His physical body and we in ours. We share Job's hope, "For I know that my redeemer liveth, and that he shall stand at the latter day upon the earth: And though after my skin worms destroy this body, yet in my flesh shall I see God" (Job 19:25, 26).

We base our hope on the past work of Jesus in the body. And we focus our eyes on the future hope of seeing Him in a body, yet in the present we struggle with this body, our physical frame. What does the Bible really say about our physical bodies? And how do our bodies measure up against the standards of Scripture? How do we relate our present Christian life to the bodies we live in? Thankfully, God is not silent on this issue.

With this Bible study you will learn to view your physical body from God's point of view, to weigh yourself by the scale of His Word. You will be encouraged to get involved in a "fitness routine."

You may be interested to know that a couple of fitness terms are actually Bible terms. Paul told the Philippians to "work out" their own salvation, reminding them it was their responsibility to grow in the Lord and in obedience to His Word. And you might remember Belshazzar in Daniel's day, a proud king who exalted himself against the Lord. The handwriting on the wall declared him to be "weighed" and "found wanting" (Daniel 5:27). God had weighed Belshazzar, and God weighs, or evaluates, what we do in our bodies as well.

May we be "fit" for His service!

# How to Use This Study

Each lesson in this study is divided into four sections—a spiritual fitness routine. Give at least three days a week to the study of each lesson. Follow these suggestions as you prepare.

## Fitness Goal

Read the fitness goal for the lesson and answer the questions to yourself alone. Think about this goal as you go through the Warm Up, Work Out, and Weigh In sections.

## Warm Up

Take one day to read the introduction and to write out the verse to memorize. This section helps you become familiar with the week's topic. Read the Work Out passages and begin to memorize the key verse.

## Work Out

Divide the Work Out questions into a two-day study. This section requires you to look more closely at a particular Bible passage. Read the passage and answer the questions, looking for what God says about the body.

## Weigh In

Visit the Weigh In questions throughout the week. This section provides opportunities to evaluate yourself by the Scriptural principles you are learning.

As you Weigh In, you will evaluate where you stand in relation to a particular Bible truth you have studied. Identify the things you should learn or attitudes or actions you should change in relation to your body. Replay the thoughts and re-pray the prayers, applying God's Word to your life.

## Pulse Check

Throughout the book are short time-outs called Pulse Check. These provide a moment for you to take in and think about what you have been learning. These questions do not require written responses.

# My Body, His Treasure

*"So God created man in his own image, in the image of God created he him; male and female created he them" (Genesis 1:27).*

### FITNESS GOAL

I will realize my value simply because I was made in the image of God. *Who am I? And does anybody care?*

From the moment we hold a precious newborn in our arms, until the day we put the precious body of a loved one into the grave, we love these bodies made of flesh. We cannot think of a person without his or her body. Since we know that the body is precious, why are we often so uncomfortable with the bodies God gave us? Could it be that something or someone has distorted our view of reality? Could it be that this discomfort is inherent with fallen humanity?

Throughout these lessons, you will examine God's purposes for your body. You will wrestle to get your feelings in line with God's truth, since your feelings about yourself often affect your actions. Specifically, how you feel about your body often reflects how you feel about yourself. Your image of yourself can affect how you behave in public, the challenges you may undertake, and even the Christian ministries you may decide to try. You may opt out of God-given opportunities because of a faulty body consciousness. Thus, failure to *conform* may keep you from being able to *perform* as God desires.

Therefore, it is important that you know God's view of your body. Rather than evaluate, or weigh, yourself by a set of standards in the media and come up short, you can weigh yourself by God's standards and accept yourself as God sees you, a woman of value created by Him.

9

## WARM UP

Write out Genesis 1:27 and begin committing it to memory.

**Read Daniel 5.**

1. a. What did Daniel remind the king about his breath (v. 23)?

    b. How did the king "weigh in" by God's standards (v. 27)?
       Note: "Wanting" in Daniel 5:27 means "lacking."

In the case of King Belshazzar, we find that weight involved a lot more than pounds on a scale. God weighed Belshazzar according to His own spiritual standard.

Society, on the other hand, weighs (or appraises) people by earthly standards, sometimes causing Christian women to lose sight of God's standards for their lives. Everywhere a woman looks, she is bombarded by pressures to conform to human standards for her body.

2. How do magazines and TV ads try to set the standards, or image, for the female body? List three examples.

3. Women often struggle with aging, anorexia, bulimia, disease, sex, style, or weight. How do these problems relate to a woman's view of herself and the pressure to maintain an ideal image?

4. According to Genesis 1:27, in whose image did God create woman?

# WORK OUT

## God's Image
### Read Genesis 1—3.

*First, being created in God's image gives people value.* God stamped His image on His human creation from the very beginning. It is this special act of creation and God's image that we bear as humans that give us purpose and value. Though God is spirit and His image within our bodies is not a physical entity, He created our bodies with enough complexity to be able to express His image. No mere animal can accomplish this.

*Second, being created in God's image gives people the ability to have fellowship.* God gave to men and women three attributes that belong to Him: will, emotion, and intellect. This means that human beings have the ability to make decisions, to express feeling, and to reason. We also have the ability to enunciate our thoughts and feelings. In the Garden, Adam and Eve were able to communicate verbally with God and with each other. They could have fellowship, communicate, share ideas with each other, make decisions, and respond emotionally to their environment.

*Third, being created in God's image involves the ability to manage, or have dominion over, creation.* This ability reflects God's right to rule. One of the first responsibilities God gave to the man and woman was to have dominion over what He had created (Genesis 1:26).

God gave mankind a wonderful pattern and privilege right from the start. We have every reason to be thankful and filled with awe at the wonder of all of His creation, but especially His creation of our own selves. Dr. Greg Couser asked the question, "What makes a body somebody?" and answered it this way: "Biblically, it is the image of God. Every person bears this image. . . . The image of God conveys value upon us as human beings and equips us for the enormous responsibility to be stewards over the world and ourselves, in order to reflect glory back on our loving Creator."[1]

    1. What thoughts in Psalm 8 indicate the value that God places on man?

## God's Person

Our key verse, Genesis 1:27, shows us something else about the image of God. When we read, "God said, Let us make man in our image" (v. 26), we hear one person speaking to others, indicating that more than one person was involved in creation. Under normal circumstances, if there's more than one person, there's more than one image, but this verse reveals something unusual: a plurality in the image of God.

2. How does Colossians 2:9 help us understand this plurality?



Bible scholars have used the word "Trinity" to describe God, because throughout the Bible three Persons are acknowledged as God: the Father, the Son, and the Holy Spirit. We also find these same three Persons active at the time of Creation.

3. Read the following passages and identify which Person of the Godhead is being credited with Creation.
   Genesis 1:2

   Genesis 2:7

   Exodus 20:11

   Job 33:4

   John 1:2

   Hebrews 1:8–10

## God's Affirmation

An eternal form of fellowship was going on inside the Trinity before God created man. God wasn't lonely. He didn't need man. Instead, He wanted man to experience fellowship with Him.

4. In Genesis 1:31, what did God conclude about all of His creation?

## PULSE CHECK

Do you always sense your value to God? Do you identify with the glory and honor with which He has crowned you?

As indicated earlier, somewhere along the line, Christian women may start viewing their bodies differently than God views them. In Genesis 3 we discover why.

The enemy of God and man visited the Garden of Eden.

5. How did Satan plant doubt about God's word, as recorded in Genesis 3:1? Note: Read Revelation 12:9 if you have any doubt about who the serpent was.


6. Read Genesis 3:4–6. How did Satan's temptation appeal to Eve's physical body?



Satan uses the same tactic today. He continues to plant doubts about God's Word in people's minds. And that holds true for the way a Christian woman feels about her body, as well. If he cannot directly attack the body, he will cause her to doubt God's design of her body by undermining her feelings and emotions about it. And he may very well use a woman's own desires to stimulate her to sin.

Sin had an immediate effect on Adam's and Eve's physical bodies.

7. According to Genesis 3:16–19, how would the punishment for their sin directly affect their bodies?



Sin distorted the image of God that Adam and Eve bore. As a result of sin, they experienced spiritual death. At this point the unhindered communication they had enjoyed with God was broken.

But sin also affected how Adam and Eve felt about their bodies.

Value Yourself– coz you are created
(worth)          in God's image.

8. How did Adam and Eve's feelings change toward their bodies from before sin to after? Compare Genesis 2:25 with 3:7–10.




Sin brought a new kind of body consciousness to man. And God responded to this new body consciousness.

## God's Intervention

In addition to confronting and condemning Adam and Eve's sin, God cared for their bodies by covering them with animal skins that cost an animal its life. This would not be the last time an animal would give its life to demonstrate the death penalty resulting from sin.

Beyond caring for their temporal need, God protected Adam and Eve from an eternal state of separation from Him by removing them from the Garden and the tree of life. Instead, He told them of His plan to crush the seed of the serpent through a seed He would give to the woman. This was God's first step in His ultimate plan for redeeming the bodies of believers. He would even use Adam and Eve's physical bodies as the human ancestors of that Seed.

After Adam and Eve left the Garden, Satan continued his attack on people and their bodies. God has devoted an entire book to a man named Job, who endured a direct Satanic attack on his body (Job 2). How Job responded to and wrestled with God during this difficult time is recorded for our learning.

9. a. How did Satan attack Job's body (Job 2:7)?



b. What did Satan conclude about such an attack (Job 2:3–7)?



10. According to Job 10:8–12 and 19:25 and 26, in spite of his infirmity, what assurances did Job have about his body?

11. Read Psalms 119:73 and 139:13–16.

a. What assurances did the psalmist have about the human body?

b. How does this truth reassure you?

## God's Investment

When God first made His covenant with Abraham, He provided for the Children of Israel a concrete lesson about the importance of their bodies: He required a literal mark in their bodies to show that they belonged to Him.

12. According to Genesis 17:11–13, what was the sign God required in their bodies? *Forskin   Incision*

13. In the New Testament, Paul explained that God no longer requires a physical sign in believers' physical bodies. However, in Galatians 6:17, Paul said he carried marks in his body. Read 2 Corinthians 6:5 and 11:24 and 25. What marks did he bear? *— Scars*

While we do not need to be circumcised and may not bear physical scars, God still wants our bodies to evidence a real connection to the Lord Jesus. In the coming lessons, we will look for some of the ways God wants believers' bodies to evidence this connection.

God shows believers how much He values them by the marks the Son bears in His body.

14. According to 1 Corinthians 15:3 and 4, what happened to Christ's body?

15. Read Galatians 4:4–6. How did God use a woman's body to redeem our human bodies?

16. In 1 Peter 1:17–19, what do you learn about the price of our redemption?

17. From 1 Peter 2:24, how did the Son of God use His body to rescue us from our problem with sin?

God has a double claim on believers' bodies. First, God made and fashioned them. Then He bought them back. All three Persons of the Trinity had a part in both their creation and their redemption.

Let's not fool ourselves. If God cares this much about our bodies, Satan targets our bodies every way he can. Just as he entered God's creation in the beginning to mar the image God had made by bringing sin into the world, so he continues to attack the body and distort the image to prevent God's image from being seen clearly.

As Satan deceived Eve and brought death to God's creation, including the human body, and as Satan later thought he could destroy Christ's body on the cross, he tries to destroy the testimony of Christ's followers by attacking their fleshly bodies. Remember Job. In Satan's attempt to get Job to turn from God, Satan went after Job's body. But don't think only of disease, death, and dying. Satan is quite content to use warm, living, healthy bodies as well—anything to get believers' focus off God.

## WEIGH IN

1. Take your Bible, book, and pen and get alone in front of a mirror. Look at your body. What do you see? What do you think about what you see?

2. How do you feel about yourself most of the time? Check the statements that apply.
   \_\_\_\_ I feel like a failure.

____ I feel worthless.

____ I feel like a shadow that most people don't notice or care about.

____ I feel self-confident and strong.

____ I feel good about myself.

____ I feel honest about myself. I try to view myself as God sees me.

____ (Other) _____
_____.

3. Have you recognized that sin is the cause of a lot of human discomfort? Have you ever acknowledged your need of having Jesus create new life in you—new eternal life?
4. If you are a believer, ask God to show you how you might do a better job of revealing His image in you. Ask God to help you see yourself as He sees you, not as the world sees you.
5. What verses can you think about when you feel an unhealthy dissatisfaction with your body?

**Note**
1. Greg Couser, "What Makes a Body Somebody?" *Torch* (Spring–Summer 2007), 15.

# My Body, His Tapestry

*"Favour is deceitful, and beauty is vain: but a woman that feareth the LORD, she shall be praised" (Proverbs 31:30).*

## FITNESS GOAL

I will accept God's standard of beauty and strive to be as beautiful as He created me to be. *What about beauty? Does God care how I look?*

The quest for beauty fuels the spending of millions of dollars each year in cosmetics, creams, anti-aging formulas, clothes, diet plans, and fitness programs. Yet few women ever reach a point where they are truly satisfied with the results.

One thing every woman knows only too well: beauty is passing. Women usually strive to look their best, even though they might not claim to aim for beauty. In fact, some almost shrink from that word. Yet in their inner-most beings, most women want to be beautiful.

But physical beauty also tends to spark comparisons. Isn't that why we have beauty pageants? In these contests, judges have tried to push the definition of beauty beyond the outward appearance. Skill, talent, and personality are measured, because intuitively, we know that beauty goes beyond the outward appearance. Yet even if a woman has never entered a contest, her sense of whether she is beautiful is often influenced by the opinions of others.

God designed beauty. Therefore, it has to be good. The problem comes when people have a different standard for beauty from God's and do not see the beauty God intends. Ask yourself, Do I "weigh in" as beautiful by Bible standards?

## WARM UP
Write out Proverbs 31:30 and begin committing it to memory.

1. List the qualities that should be included in a definition of "beauty." For example, my husband would say that "beauty always smiles."

One of the first things you will notice when you look for beautiful women in the Bible is that there are few of them. Of the 193 women, fewer than 20 are referred to as beautiful in appearance; that is less than 1 out of 10.

2. Use the chart below to record the answers to these questions: Who were some of the beauties in the Bible? What else, if anything, is noted with their beauty? Who noted their beauty?

| Reference | Name | What Else Is Noted | Who Noted It |
|---|---|---|---|
| Genesis 12:11, 14, 15 | | | |
| Genesis 24:2, 11–21, 58, 64, 67 | | | |
| Genesis 29:16–20 | | | |
| 1 Samuel 25:3, 32–42 | | | |
| 2 Samuel 11:2–5 | | | |
| Esther 1:11–13, 15–19 | | | |
| Esther 2:7–9, 15–17 | | | |
| Someone you want to mention. Provide Scripture references. | | | |

3. Considering each woman in the chart, how much did it profit each lady to be physically beautiful?

Two other women of the Bible, Ruth and the Proverbs 31 woman, are often thought to be beautiful, though a closer look does not find the word for beauty describing either one. Instead, the Bible refers to both as virtuous (Ruth 3:11; Proverbs 31:10).

    4. Compare the dictionary definitions of "beauty" or "beautiful" with "virtuous."

## WORK OUT

**Read Ruth 1:16, 2:11 and 12, and 3:11 and Proverbs 31.**

    1. What beautiful behavior qualities do you find in both Ruth and the Proverbs 31 woman?

| Ruth | Proverbs 31 Woman |
|------|-------------------|
|      |                   |

In 1 Samuel 16:1–13, the Bible records a story that reveals what beauty is from God's point of view, even though the story has no women in it. God asked Samuel to select one of the eight sons of Jesse to be the king after Saul. Jesse brought his sons before Samuel, beginning with the oldest. Samuel apparently checked out the man's physical appearance, including his height, and thought, "Surely the Lord's anointed is before Him!" That's when God clarified the issue for Samuel.

    2. Read 1 Samuel 16:1–13.

        a. How did God describe the criterion for His choice of king, according to 1 Samuel 16:7?

b. How does this criterion compare to the standard in Proverbs
   31:30?


Believers are not to use outward appearance as the main criterion by
which to evaluate the women of the Bible, or anyone else, for that matter.
Outward beauty is not bad. God designed beauty. However, mere humans
do not have the advantage God has. They cannot see a person's heart or
motives. Believers ought to accept the caution that physical appearance
does not tell everything about a person. Though physical appearance is
important to people, it is not God's standard for evaluation.


### PULSE CHECK
Whose opinions of beauty do you value? Do you ever
make assumptions about other people based on
externals?

Whether we like it or not, people judge one another by outward appearances. Believers have to decide to be different, to see people as God
sees them. You may remember that being judged by outward appearances
caused the apostle Paul grief among the Corinthians. This may be why
Paul's letters to the Corinthians say more about the body than any of his
other letters. Accordingly, several lessons can be drawn from Paul's writings and specifically from 1 and 2 Corinthians.

3. What had the Corinthians been saying about Paul's appearance,
   according to 2 Corinthians 10:10?


4. How had Paul cautioned them in 1 Corinthians 4:7 to understand
   the differences they saw in one another?

5. In spite of differences in appearance or talent among believers, what special uniqueness do all believers share, according to 1 Corinthians 3:16 and 6:19?


## Appearance

Though Paul did not use the term "beauty," he did address the dangers of comparing external characteristics. Whether our differences show up in talents or in personal appearance, Paul said believers have nothing personally to boast about; anything they have or are is from God.

Shape and height, texture and color are determined by the amazing genes that the Lord implanted in you as He designed you in the womb. These were His gifts to you. Be assured that God likes what He created you to be, in all of your physical features. You are beautiful to Him. You please Him! You meet the definition of beauty: "the quality of being very pleasing, as in form, color, tone, behavior, etc."

As with every gift, you have a responsibility to care for that gift. Diet, exercise, nutrition, cosmetics, clothing, and cleanliness all influence external beauty. For example, color and texture might determine the use of cosmetics. Height and weight may affect the choice of clothing. But the first step in caring for our bodies begins with accepting what God has given us.

6. How did the Proverbs 31 woman care for her body to enhance her appearance? See verses 16–27.


7. How did Naomi advise Ruth when she sent her to Boaz (Ruth 3:3)?


8. According to 1 Peter 3:3 and 4, what kind of adornment is precious in the sight of God?


Thus, while women can learn to enhance outward beauty, they dare not forget that to God, nothing enhances beauty like the heart attitude.

## Diet

Because diet and exercise are often misunderstood, these two areas
will be discussed in this section. Diet and exercise do not determine basic
shape; they can only tighten or improve bodies to a certain extent. A woman's God-given genes not only determine shape and appearance, but they
influence the effect that diet or exercise will have on her body. That is why
different people lose or gain weight in different places.

Diet and food choices differ for people, depending on their bodies'
needs and differing metabolisms. Beyond this, Christian women must be
careful to keep their emphasis on diet in perspective with other requirements that God has for believers. A misguided emphasis on diet can lead
to problems such as bulimia or anorexia. Anita Young, in her Bible study
*Becoming the Noble Woman*, suggested that while "nutrition has become
an area of interest to most Americans . . . it can also become another
obsession."[1] She cautioned that gluttony can be a problem for both the
overweight and the underweight: "Gluttony allows your appetite and tastes
to rule what, when, and how much you eat, and takes over your life. Additional food disorders, anorexia and bulimia, as well as gluttony, put the
concern about food way out of proportion to your needs. An obsession with
food can lead to undernourishment for the sake of attaining an unhealthy,
underweight body."[2]

From the beginning (Genesis 1:29, 30; 2:15–17), God provided all kinds
of fruits and vegetables for people to eat. And then, after the Flood, He
added meat (Genesis 9:1–4).

    9. What caution did God give about eating and drinking? See Prov-
       erbs 23:20 and 21.


Some people read the dietary laws written for the Jewish nation in
Leviticus, Numbers, and Deuteronomy and try to come up with a diet for
today. They suggest that many of these dietary laws were given for health
reasons, especially to protect a nomadic people who did not have refrigera-
tion and other ways to protect themselves from the spread of disease.

However, part of the purpose of the Jewish diet was to keep the Jewish nation a separate and holy people. For example, in Exodus 34:15, God

cautioned His people that they should not make a covenant with idolaters or eat meat that was sacrificed to their idols. God chose to create a new nation, a people from whom He would bless the world by sending His Son to be their Savior. He also gave them a set of laws that would make them a unique people. Some of these laws included their diet.

In the New Testament we learn that the Levitical food requirements were temporary. In Acts 10:9–16, God showed Peter various unclean animals and told him to eat. That day Gentile visitors knocked on Peter's door. God used food to teach Peter that God wanted to save Gentiles as well as Jews. But Peter also learned that the old Jewish food requirements were no longer necessary.

**Read 1 Timothy 4:4–6.**

    10. What guideline for eating did Paul give in 4:4?

    11. What kind of nourishment did Paul think is most important, according to 4:6?

    12. Jesus was tempted by Satan (Matthew 4:4). How did His response exemplify what Paul taught in 4:6?

    13. Romans 14 and 1 Corinthians 8 provide other principles or guidelines for eating. They emphasize that relationships with people are more important than specific food choices. Write one of these principles in your own words and note which verse or verses this principle comes from.

    14. According to 1 Corinthians 10:31, what overriding principle should be a believer's main concern even when eating?

Eating well-balanced meals that satisfy nutritional needs makes Biblical sense. However, God cares about more than the calorie-count of food; God cares about His children's relationships to others. When a woman is consumed with herself and her body, she will seldom notice the needs of those around her. Beyond using food for nourishment, God uses the body's need for food and exercise to teach believers what is most important to Him—His Word and His people.

## Exercise

Rules similar to those for diet can be applied to exercise or any other area of life, but it can be helpful to look at a few verses that mention exercise specifically.

15. In 1 Corinthians 9:23–26, Paul referred to the body and exercise.
    a. What kinds of athletes did Paul mention?

    b. How did he apply their discipline to his life?

16. a. What did Paul say about exercise in 1 Timothy 4:7 and 8?

    b. What kind of exercise did he say is most important?

17. So while dress, food, and exercise are important to the physical body, what should be a Christian woman's main concern when it comes to beauty, according to Proverbs 31:30?

A woman's dress, food, and exercise must glorify God, but He has a higher purpose for the body. God is more interested in our spiritual nourishment and exercise unto godliness because He looks on the inside. He cares about inner beauty.

Becoming overly concerned about externals—appearance, weight, health, age—tells people that only this temporal life counts. But balancing care for the external with care (food and exercise) for the internal shows that the Christian woman weighs by a different standard—that she has an interest in the eternal.

God shaped you for beauty—inner and outer. He designed your outer beauty in the womb and in His perfect plan. Now He is developing your inner beauty as you seek His glory through His Word. Ask Him to help you be beautiful—inside and outside—so He gets the glory.

## WEIGH IN

1. How do you see yourself? Whose standard do you use to decide if you are beautiful in appearance? Whose opinion do you value most?
2. How beautiful are you on the inside? What does God see that others may not see?
3. Pray Psalm 90:17 with the psalmist: "And let the beauty of the LORD our God be upon us: and establish thou the work of our hands upon us; yea, the work of our hands establish thou it."
4. Sing this song to the Lord:
   *"Let the beauty of Jesus be seen in me,*
   *All His wonderful passion and purity—*
   *O Thou Spirit, divine, All my nature refine,*
   *Till the beauty of Jesus be seen in me."*
   **—Albert Orsbon**

**Notes**

1. Anita Young, *Becoming the Noble Woman* (Tulsa: Hensley Publishing, 1988), 51.
2. Ibid.

# My Body, His Reflection

*"According to my earnest expectation and my hope, that in nothing I shall be ashamed, but that with all boldness, as always, so now also Christ shall be magnified in my body, whether it be by life, or by death. For to me to live is Christ, and to die is gain" (Philippians 1:20, 21).*

**FITNESS GOAL**

I will accept the physical limitations I have, or think I have, and trust God to use them for the furtherance of His gospel and for His glory in the church. *How can God use me?*

All people have limitations to some extent. Some may not have the education they wish they had. Many consider themselves to be too short or too tall, too fat or too skinny. Others may have physical limitations that hinder them from doing a particular activity.

Author Jerry Bridges, in his book *Trusting God,* describes a visual disability he has that hindered his ability to play ball well in elementary school. This made him feel inferior to the other boys at an age when success in sports seemed very important.

Bridges did not know until much later that he had monocular vision, which hindered his depth perception. Now he understands his problem and has learned to accept this limitation. However, as a young person, he "felt shame and rejection." He wrote, "Of course, many people have physical or mental impairments that are much worse than mine. But whether they are major or minor, these disabilities often cause childhood heartache and then, later on, difficulty with self-acceptance as an adult."[1]

As a prisoner, the apostle Paul had limitations of a different sort. He was in prison, chained to guards, and his friends at Philippi were worried about him. They were genuinely concerned about his well-being and the bonds, or chains, that held his body. So Paul wrote to let them know he understood and appreciated their concern for his bodily comforts and needs, as well as for their own physical suffering. He didn't ignore this important facet of life, as though the body doesn't matter. Bodies do hurt, feel pain, and suffer deprivation. Paul recognized that it is quite natural for people to be concerned about their physical bodies first. But Paul wanted to direct their focus back on target, not on his predicament or theirs, but on how God would be glorified through personal limitations.

## WARM UP

Write out Philippians 1:20 and 21 and begin committing these verses to memory.

Read Acts 16:11–38. Then read the letter to the Philippians and underline the references that pertain to the physical body. Notice that Paul discussed his own physical situation in chapter 1, gave examples of people who used their bodies for God in chapter 2, discussed ultimate goals for the body in chapter 3, and gave some practical admonitions in chapter 4.

1. According to Acts 16:11–38, how did God use Paul to begin His work among the Philippians? Who were some of the first believers in the Philippian church?

2. How was Christ magnified through the painful events mentioned in Acts 16:23–34?

3. In Philippians 1:3–5 Paul expressed gratitude for the partnership of the Philippian church in spreading the gospel. According to Philippians 4:10 and 14–18, how had the Philippians encouraged Paul?

## WORK OUT

Though Paul was in chains, he was more concerned for the Philippians than he was for himself. Paul used his circumstances to help them see that physical limitations do not limit God; they simply give Him the opportunity to work through Christians in a much grander way. Though Paul's body was literally chained, he rejoiced because the gospel was not chained. Paul's personal goal was to magnify Christ. And he didn't really care whether it was by his life or by his death—just so Christ was truly magnified.

## Chains Bring Spiritual Gain
### Reread Philippians 1.

1. How did Paul pray for his friends, as recorded in 1:9–11?


2. How did Paul's chains benefit the gospel, according to 1:12 and 13?


3. According to 1:14 and 15, how had his chains encouraged "the brethren," or fellow believers?


4. Why did Paul rejoice in his chains, according to 1:16–18?


5. Paul kept the gospel at the center of his life in spite of his chains. Find the six times he mentioned the gospel in Philippians 1, and record the phrase he used about the gospel and any reference to chains. An example is provided (p. 32).

| Reference in Philippians | Mention of the Gospel and Bonds | Summary |
|---|---|---|
| 1:5 | "your fellowship in the gospel" | Paul was thankful for the Philippians' fellowship in the gospel. |

6. How does Colossians 4:2–4 express Paul's passion for the gospel?


It is not surprising that the bulk of believers' prayer requests concern their physical bodies. This is natural. Our bodies go with us all the time. In fact, we can't live apart from our bodies. The physical condition of our bodies often affects what we believers are able to do for the Lord.

Paul appreciated the prayers of the Philippians for him. He didn't want them to stop praying for him and for his deliverance, or "salvation" (Philippians 1:19), but he also wanted them to pray wisely and to understand what was most important.

7. Rather than his chains, what was Paul's main concern for his body? See Philippians 1:20.


8. a. According to 1:21, what was Paul's reason for living?

b. Why was he not afraid to die?

### PULSE CHECK

What physical, situational, or emotional limitations do you have? Have you ever asked the Lord to use this particular weakness or drawback to help you share the gospel with someone? Have you ever asked someone to pray that God would use this limitation for His glory?

9. a. According to 1:22–26, what struggle did Paul have within himself?

   b. What does this tell you about Paul's concern for other believers?

10. a. Below, list Paul's goals for the Philippians as recorded in 1:27 and 28.
    b. Below, compare these goals with his prayer request for them in 1:9–11.

| Goals | Prayer Requests |
|---|---|
|  |  |

11. Why might the Philippians have needed Paul's example and encouragement? See Philippians 1:29 and 30.

## Loss and Limitations Turned to Gain
**Reread Philippians 2.**

Suffering of any kind is not easy. Paul knew that a person's response to suffering begins in the mind; therefore, he began Philippians 2 with a reference to his readers' minds. Right thinking works itself out in right actions. He pointed his friends to the comfort they had in Christ, Who also had lived in a physical body. Paul told them they must think as Christ thought and must be of one mind, Christ's kind of mind. Then Paul described the way Christ thought and acted.

12. How did Christ accept and even welcome limitations, according to 2:5–11?

13. Paul reminded the Philippians that it was God Who worked in them. How, in turn, did Paul expect them to "work out" their salvation, according to 2:12–16?

14. Read Philippians 2:19–30 and explain how Timothy and Epaphroditus exemplified right thinking that led to right action. In other words, how did each use his body to serve the Lord and the Philippians?
Timothy

Epaphroditus

## Gain Turned to Loss
### Reread Philippians 3.

Some people may limit their potential by thinking too lowly of themselves because of their limitations, but others may limit their potential by thinking too highly of themselves. People in this situation may boast about their family ties, their children, their education, their shape, their health, etc. Instead of finding satisfaction in any type of worldly status or success, each believer must depend on Christ. In Philippians 3:4–6, Paul listed his credentials, which some people would boast about. But he counted them all loss for Christ, "for the excellency of the knowledge of Christ Jesus my Lord" (3:8).

15. According to Philippians 3:10 and following, what did Paul want to gain?


16. According to Paul in 3:18 and 19, what do the enemies of the cross of Christ expect to gain?


17. Read 3:20 and 21. What is the ultimate goal for the body of a believer?


Believers live in limited physical bodies, but God has a divine purpose for those bodies. His children can focus on their bodies and their limitations, or they can allow their limited bodies to magnify Christ. Paul encouraged the Philippians because they also had been suffering for the gospel, and he wanted them to recognize that their struggles, their persecutions, even their chains might be their opportunity to magnify God's Son. Paul assured his readers that even limitations have a purpose—magnifying Christ and giving Him more glory.

God can take every loss or limitation, including every *physical* loss or limitation, and use it for His glory. In fact, none of what someone thinks is "gain" can be used for God unless it is first counted loss and given to Him. Often the very limitations believers have that make them look smaller or feel weaker are used to make Christ loom larger. Believers may be concerned that their limitations hinder the spread of the gospel, when in actuality they help to hide believers and turn the focus where it should be—on Christ.

## WEIGH IN

1. How can you balance concern for your body with your desire to magnify Christ in your body? After writing your thoughts, check Philippians 4:6–13.

2. How would Paul answer the question, "What is the purpose for life?" Do you agree with Paul's answer? If not, why not? Ask the Lord to help you view your life and purpose as He wants you to.

3. Reflect on your personal weaknesses. Praise the Lord for any chance He has given you to help or encourage someone because of your own physical or emotional limitations.

4. With Paul, are you willing to acknowledge that your "chains"— weaknesses, illnesses, inadequacies, limitations—are your opportunity to magnify His Son? Write a prayer in your own words, acknowledging a limitation and asking God to use that limitation for His glory.

**Note**

1. Jerry Bridges, *Trusting God: Even When Life Hurts* (Colorado Springs: NavPress, 1990), 160.

# My Body, His Tablet

*"But we all, with open face beholding as in a glass the glory* ~~1st~~:
*of the Lord, are changed into the same image from glory* _Salvation_
*to glory, even as by the Spirit of the Lord" (2 Corinthians* ~~2nd~~

*3:18).* Final Glory:
— Total Glorification (as if I don't

John 17:17 — Find a time   3rd sin)

**FITNESS GOAL** to Read   justified

God's word   sanctified

I will be aware that my lifestyle, or my everyday pat-  (set apart
tern of living, sends a message to the world about — to be a
Christ. *What will it say? Does it show others the power* testimony
*of God in my life?*   to see Christ

hat you do speaks so loud, I can't hear what you say!" As these
words indicate, the physical body speaks a language of sorts. It's
called "body language." As you know, body language is important. Though not as precise as verbal language, nonverbal language still
communicates. Facial expressions, gestures, and body movement convey
messages. Sometimes body language gives one message, while verbal language gives another. For instance, if I say, "This food tastes delicious!" but
then don't eat it or wrinkle my nose at it, the cook gets a mixed message.
She probably won't believe what I said. Therefore, it is important that body
language reinforces verbal language. If you say you love Christ, it is important that your body language affirms what Christ means to you.

Not only do your actions affirm or deny your verbal claims, but the
emphasis you place on your body can evidence your real concerns. Your
actions, plans, speech, and perhaps even your wardrobe can speak loudly
to either enhance your witness for Christ or distort the message you try to
portray about Christ. What do your body language and actions say about
Christ to those around you? That was one of Paul's concerns in much of
1 and 2 Corinthians. In 2 Corinthians, Paul described the body using three

Always a picture of Christ!

37

metaphors: a tablet, a vessel, and a tent. This lesson looks at the believer's body as a writing tablet.

## WARM UP

Write out 2 Corinthians 3:18 and begin committing it to memory.

1. Tell about a time when someone's nonverbal body language did not match his or her verbal language. What conflicting messages did you receive?

2. People are sometimes described as an "open book." What does that mean?

Paul used a similar analogy to the "open book" in 2 Corinthians 3 when he told the Corinthians that they were epistles (or letters) written with the ink of the Holy Spirit on the tablets of their hearts. Dorothy Kelley Patterson, in her book *BeAttitudes for Women,* made a similar comparison when she said, "Women who bear the name of Christ must remember that in a sense they are writing a book through the way they live their daily lives."[1]

## WORK OUT

### A Letter Read by All
**Read 2 Corinthians 3:1–12.**

In this chapter the apostle Paul discussed the use of reference letters. He began by explaining why such a letter was unnecessary in his ministry.

1. a. What is the purpose of a reference letter?

b. Have you ever written a reference letter for someone?

2. In 3:1, how did Paul describe these letters?

3. a. According to verses 2 and 3, what was unique about these letters?

b. What type of "stationery" was used for these letters?

4. What do you think Paul meant when he said that the Corinthians became known and read by all men (v. 2)?

Paul wrote many letters to churches and individuals. But he also wrote other letters in the hearts and lives of people. Not only were the Corinthians a reference letter for Paul and his ministry, but Paul's own life was a reference letter for the gospel. God had changed Paul from chief persecutor of the Christians to passionate preacher of the gospel. In a similar way today, you are a reference letter or testimony to the New Testament message of salvation. You show the genuineness of the gospel message by your life.

### PULSE CHECK
What kind of reference are you for Christ and the gospel?

## A Letter Made Possible by Christ

Living to accurately translate the gospel to people is a huge responsibility, but believers are not on their own. Second Corinthians 3:4–12 teaches believers that their confidence must come through Christ and their sufficiency must come from God. Paul wanted the Corinthians to understand that through Christ, God has made them ministers of a new "testament" or "covenant." Therefore, carrying out this responsibility is not simply about teaching people to do good or keep the Ten Commandments, but about depending on the Holy Spirit to live life in Christ as we should. At the Last Supper, Christ took the cup and said, "This cup is the new testament in my blood" (1 Corinthians 11:25). Paul's message is about Christ shedding His blood for our sins. In contrast to the law of Moses, which only condemned, this new covenant provides salvation by faith apart from works, for both Jews and Gentiles.

5. Use the chart below to contrast the two covenants by looking at Paul's and Moses' ministries. What does 2 Corinthians 3:6–12 identify as differences?

| Paul's Ministry | Moses' Ministry |
| --- | --- |
| 1. Tablets of _Heart_ | 1. Tablets of _Stones_ |
| Comparisons Continued— | |
| 2. | 2. |
| 3. | 3. |
| 4. life / kills | 4. |
| 5. ministry of spirit | 5. death |
| 6. Righteousness | 6. ministry of death / condemnation |

## An Unveiled Letter
### Read 2 Corinthians 3:14–18.

Empowered by the Holy Spirit, believers are "letters" for unbelievers to read. But there's a problem.

6. What do John 12:40 and 2 Corinthians 3:14 and 4:4 indicate about the spiritual eyes of unbelievers?

7. What problem do 2 Corinthians 3:14 and 15 identify?

8. According to 2 Corinthians 3:16, who or what can solve this problem?

People can't do anything to take the veil of unbelief off the eyes of others. The Holy Spirit removes the veils as believers "preach Christ."

The Ethiopian eunuch of Acts 8:30–37 is a good example of a person who has a veil over his or her eyes. He was reading from Isaiah 53, but he did not understand that he was reading about Jesus Christ. When Philip approached the eunuch's chariot, he began to preach Christ to the eunuch until the Holy Spirit removed the veil and the man understood and believed. The same "eye-opening" experience has happened to all sinners who have believed on Jesus as their Savior.

### PULSE CHECK
Have you turned to the Lord as personal Savior? When? Share your testimony with someone in your family or someone in your Bible study group.

The Christian life begins when the sinner is honest—open-faced, or unveiled—before God. Moved by the Holy Spirit, she takes off the veil of self-righteousness that she has tried to hide behind. And as simple as A-B-C, she *admits* that she's a sinner and cannot change herself (Romans 3:23; 6:23; Ephesians 2:8, 9; Titus 3:5); she *believes* that Jesus Christ's death on the cross and resurrection from the grave provide the only hope for her (John 3:16; Romans 4:25), and she *calls* on Christ, trusting Him to save her (Romans 10:9, 10).

When someone receives Christ as Savior, a change takes place. An old hymn says, "What a wonderful change in my life has been wrought, since Jesus came into my heart." Second Corinthians 5:17 makes it clear that the believer is given a new nature in Christ Jesus. Indeed, every believer is made a new creation.

## A Letter Changed by God and His Word
### Reread 2 Corinthians 3:18.
The Christian life is an open life that grows and changes in response to

God's Word as the Spirit works in believers. Though salvation comes in a moment, the change continues throughout life, "from glory to glory."

  9. According 2 Corinthians 3:18, what changes begin to take place after the veil has been removed?


The word "beholding" in verse 18 indicates a long gaze. As a Christian woman looks into God's Word, she can't get her eyes off what she sees. She doesn't turn away and forget. This involves some personal responsibility.

  10. James 1:22–25 helps us understand the value of the mirror of God's Word. What caution or warning is given in these verses?



  11. According to Proverbs 3:1–3, what needs to be written on our hearts?



These passages help us understand the importance of the Word of God in our lives. As we behold Christ and obey the Word of God, our lives change. When God's Word is written on the tablets of our hearts, our lives can become a tablet that other people read to learn about Christ.

## A Letter Changed by the Spirit

  12. Review our memory verse, 2 Corinthians 3:18. Who accomplishes this transforming work in us?


As believers look at the glory of the Lord in the Word, the Holy Spirit begins to change them into the image of the Lord. The result is what people call "Christlikeness." Christ's image is seen in the Word; and the Spirit gradually changes believers to be more like Christ. That is Holy Spirit transformation. Bible scholars also call this sanctification, the process by which the Holy Spirit makes Christians more holy, more like Christ.

The Greek word for "changed" in 2 Corinthians 3:18 provides a clear picture of what takes place, because it comes from the same root word as the English word "metamorphosis." When a caterpillar spins a chrysalis and then emerges as a beautiful butterfly, it has gone through metamorphosis. It is completely transformed into a new and beautiful creature, able to do things that it could never have done as a worm or lowly caterpillar. God wants to change believers' lowly "worm-like" lives into the glorious "butterfly-type" image of Himself.

Paul used this picture to explain to believers how our bodies can become tablets on which the gospel can be read by other people. As people see our changing lifestyles, they will want to know what caused the change.

13. a. According to 2 Corinthians 4:1 and 2, how did the ministry of the Spirit affect Paul's life and ministry?


b. How would the Spirit's ministry help Paul to commend himself "to every man's conscience" (2 Corinthians 4:2)?


Unsaved people are strangers, or foreigners, to God. They cannot speak His language; therefore, they cannot understand or know Him. But as the Holy Spirit changes us from glory to glory, we believers in Christ can translate or interpret for the unsaved. This does not happen simply by our words, but also by our lives or our body language.

Sadly, however, Christians too often give one message with their words and another with their bodies. If Christians forget what they see in the mirror (God's Word), if they fail to write those words on the tablets of their hearts, they may verbalize with words that they love the Lord, but their "body language" may tell people that they love something else even more. The closer God's people get to measuring up to Bible standards, the more accurately their body language will reinforce what their words say. Believers can and should give a clear, accurate presentation of God.

## WEIGH IN

1. What kind of first impressions do you make? With people you know well, what are you known for?

2. Does your behavior veil the gospel to people? Or can they see clearly that the Holy Spirit is really changing your life and, in fact, makes life worth living?

3. Ask God to make you an authentic Christian, to enable people to see Christ in you. Write a prayer of commitment to be a "tablet" that clearly and accurately portrays Christ.

**Note**

1. Dorothy Kelley Patterson, *BeAttitudes for Women: Wisdom from Heaven for Life on Earth* (Eugene, OR: Wipf & Stock Publishers, 2008), 180.

# My Body, His Vessel

*"But we have this treasure in earthen vessels, that the excellency of the power may be of God, and not of us" (2 Corinthians 4:7).*

### FITNESS GOAL

I will live in such a way that my physical body shows the essence of the gospel to those around me. *What do others see in me?*

In Bible times, containers were often made from clay that was shaped and baked, then used for cups, bowls, kneading troughs, pitchers, cooking pots, griddles, and washbasins. The pieces were common, ordinary, easily broken, and easily replaced. They had no value except as a tool. If the container was never used, it had no value at all. Today's lesson shows that Christian women also are vessels of clay, subject to cracking and even breakage. Each of us has her own weaknesses. We are fragile. But a clay pot is exactly what God wants to use. He sees us as we are, but wants to use us to store a very valuable treasure.

### WARM UP

Write out 2 Corinthians 4:7 and begin committing it to memory.

Why not light a fragrant candle or potpourri pot as you "warm up." Then read Gideon's story in Judges 7.

In this passage a simple pitcher was used for a unique purpose. In fact, God used it to defeat the entire host of Midianites. After God instructed Gideon to reduce the size of his army, Gideon ended up with a small group of three hundred men.

1. According to Judges 7:16, what did Gideon give each of the three hundred men?


2. What was the purpose of the pitcher?


3. In Judges 7:17–21, how were these simple pitchers strategically used in the battle?


Think about what God could accomplish through you.


## WORK OUT
### Bearing the Light
**Read 2 Corinthians 4:3–7.**

1. According to 2 Corinthians 4:3–7, what is the treasure that God wants to shine from our vessel?


2. Explain some ways in which our bodies are like earthen vessels or jars of clay.


Second Corinthians 4:3–6 likens the gospel to light shining in the darkness. As God commanded the light to shine in darkness at the beginning of Creation, and as He commanded the light to break forth among Gideon's men, so God continues to shine the light of His good news in the darkness of our present world through earthen, human vessels.

3. What is the gospel, according to 1 Corinthians 15:1–4?


My friend Pam Goller once said: "God has chosen to place Himself inside every believer! Just try to grasp that for a second—the Creator of everything beautiful and complicated and mysterious chose to live inside a container that was ordinary, flawed, and breakable."

## Spreading the Fragrance
**Read 2 Corinthians 2:12–16.**

First Corinthians 4:3–6 and Matthew 5:16 emphasize the light of the gospel, but sometimes a pot can give not only light, but fragrance.

    4. a. According to 2 Corinthians 2:12–15, what was Paul's purpose in Troas?


       b. What caused the savor, or fragrance, in that place?


    5. a. In 2:15 and 16, what were the two groups who became aware of that fragrance?


       b. What was the difference between them?


As the same flowers can be used at a wedding or a funeral, so the gospel can give life to all who receive Jesus, but it also warns of death to any who reject Jesus. The fragrance will remain the same, but the response will differ.

Linking the fragrance of the gospel witness mentioned in 2 Corinthians 2 with the light of the gospel mentioned in chapter 4, it seems appropriate to compare believers' lives to a potpourri pot. These burn a candle under a pot of liquid potpourri. As the candle heats the liquid, the fragrance of the potpourri begins to filter through the room. Some jars have fancy carvings on the sides that allow light to filter through to provide a lovely romantic ambiance. Our fragile earthen clay vessels should exude both fragrance and light. Let's look further at the vessel in 2 Corinthians 4.

## PULSE CHECK
Have you believed the gospel—that Christ died for
sin, rose again, and is now living in Heaven? Have you
accepted God's treasure? Have you come to appreciate
the fragrance of the gospel?

## Manifesting the Gospel
**Read 2 Corinthians 4:7–14.**

6. According to 2 Corinthians 4:7, why does God put a valuable treasure into such a weak vessel?

7. How does that compare to what God told Gideon in Judges 7:2?

Every year our daughter-in-law's parents saved money in a piggy bank.
At Thanksgiving, her dad would break the bank and let the kids count and
divide the money for their Christmas shopping. Everyone looked forward
to the treasure. No one cared much for the "pot." God, on the other hand,
does care for the pot, but He knows that it is only His excellent power that
can accomplish anything in our lives, not our power or ability. The un-
likely character of the pot tends to make sure that people value the treasure inside, lest we try to hide the treasure and glorify the pot.

8. Describe the pressures on these earthen vessels (2 Corinthians 4:8, 9).

9. How does 1 Corinthians 10:13 assure us that there are limits to the
pressures? If you are currently suffering or under severe pressure,
claim this verse as God's promise to you.

10. According to 2 Corinthians 4:10 and 11, what two aspects of Jesus
are shown in believers' bodies?

11. According to 2 Corinthians 4:14, how does death in Jesus ultimately bring life to our mortal bodies?


It should be comforting to note that the Christian life, with its struggles
and victories, becomes a picture of the death and life of our Savior. Somehow we always carry in our bodies the dying of the Lord Jesus, that the life
of Jesus—His powerful resurrection life—may also be seen in us.

When we believers are hard-pressed but not crushed, the life of Jesus is
made manifest. When we are perplexed but not despairing, the life of Jesus
shows through us. We may be delivered to death for Jesus' sake, but His life
is also manifest when people see that we are not forsaken. We are cared for
by a living Savior! We may even be struck down for Jesus' sake; yet because
He lives, we cannot be destroyed.

We carry the wonderful treasure of the gospel in our fragile vessels.
What is the gospel that people must understand? It is the death and resurrection of the Lord Jesus. Is it any wonder that He might want to show this
death and life principle in the vessels that He owns?

Though we may struggle to appreciate this truth, Paul seemed to understand it very well.

12. How is Paul's prayer in Philippians 3:10 unusual?


Isn't it amazing that God would so intertwine His life with ours that
our bodies could begin to speak for and of His Son? No wonder Paul said
we have a treasure in our earthen vessels! Someone has explained that our
lives are not really *transparent,* because the unsaved may never quite see
through us. But our lives can be *translucent;* that is, the light of the gospel
can show through.

Think again of the potpourri pot. The death of the Lord Jesus goes in—
we share in the sufferings of Jesus—but by His amazing grace, He works
in our struggles to bring out the fragrance of His life (2 Corinthians 2:15).
Then as God opens the eyes of others, they see the light of His glorious gospel (4:4, 6).

## Enduring the Pressure
**Read 2 Corinthians 11:22–29 and 12:7–10.**

In the later chapters of 2 Corinthians, we find a number of trials that Paul experienced for the sake of the gospel—many of them "near-death" experiences.

13. From 2 Corinthians 11:22–29 list some of the life-threatening dangers that Paul went through.

14. a. In 2 Corinthians 12:7, how did Paul describe another physical problem that he endured?

   b. What had Paul done about this physical trial, according to 2 Corinthians 12:8?

15. How did God answer Paul's prayer, according to 2 Corinthians 12:9?

16. How did Paul respond to God's answer? See 2 Corinthians 12:9 and 10.

17. In 2 Corinthians 13:4, how did Paul compare his experiences to Christ's crucifixion?

18. How do 2 Corinthians 4:15 and 13:9 explain Paul's selfless view of personal suffering?

19. Paul used the "vessel" motif in his letter to the Romans. He called those who trusted Him as Savior "the vessels of mercy" (Romans 9:23). What does God want to accomplish in His vessels of mercy?

20. Let's leave Paul's writings now and "go down to the potter's house" (Jeremiah 18:2–6). What can you learn with Jeremiah about the Lord's working in your life?

In her book *Radical Gratitude,* Ellen Vaughn tells the story of a stalled subway train. In the crowded subway car, passengers became increasingly hostile as they voiced their anger and frustration over the situation. In the midst of all the confusion, a woman with a number of bags dropped one that contained perfume. As soon as the bottle shattered, the fragrance began to permeate the car. Within minutes, the behavior of the other passengers began to improve. People began to relax, to laugh, to change their tone of voice. God wants the fragrance of the gospel to likewise escape from our lives so it will awaken people to the light of His glorious gospel. Let Him use your broken or fragile vessel to radiate the fragrance and light of His glory.

## WEIGH IN

Dab on a little perfume, or take a whiff of your fragrant potpourri pot, and think about yourself for a moment.

1. What kind of fragrance do people sense when they bump up against you?

2. Can you relate to any of the pressures that Paul mentioned? If so, briefly describe a time when you felt one of these pressures and tell how the Lord preserved you. If you are currently experiencing such pressure, how is the Lord sustaining you? Is there a verse from this lesson that you can cling to?

3. Do you feel like a marred vessel? Let God remake you; let God shape you. Let Him use you to show forth the treasure of His Son in you. If some bodily affliction concerns you—your age, your frailty,

some recurring habit—present these bodily afflictions to God and ask Him how He might use your body to show the light of this glorious gospel of Christ. Write out your prayer to God.

# My Body, His Tent

*"Always bearing about in the body the dying of the Lord Jesus, that the life also of Jesus might be made manifest in our body. For we which live are alway delivered unto death for Jesus' sake, that the life also of Jesus might be made manifest in our mortal flesh" (2 Corinthians 4:10, 11).*

## FITNESS GOAL

I will trust God during my life and in death. *Do I trust God for the big and little things in my life? Will I trust Him when the prospect of imminent death looms?*

Thank God for aging? No one would want to thank God for that. But as Dr. Charles Dolph wrote in an article on aging,

> We must not forget that there is always meaning and purpose, even in aging and illness. Aging strips us. If we live long enough, we will lose our beauty, our strength, our wealth, our independence, the control of our bodily functions, our pride, and perhaps our very self. These are our idols, all the things that we trust in life to make us attractive, valuable, and self-sufficient.
>
> If our aging is successful, we will end our lives stripped of everything but God, totally naked and helpless, utterly dependent on Him and the love of others. Everything that we trusted in life for our worth will have been stripped away.[1]

Believers should agree with the words Dr. Dolph added at the end of his article: "What a blessing to finally find our right relationship to God!

Thank God for aging."[2] This one short article packs a bundle of truth.

## WARM UP
Write out 2 Corinthians 4:10 and 11 and begin committing them to memory.

When considering death, many individuals simply place their hope in becoming part of the "eternal" world around us, or they just resign themselves to moving into nothingness. They might think it strange that Christians talk about eternal life and going to Heaven. However, they often marvel at the peace believers have as they stand by the dead bodies of their loved ones. Believers sorrow, but also thank God for His presence and sustenance during their time of great sorrow. They sing songs of faith and give glory to God. This comes only by resurrection power, the "excellency of" His power.

We have also seen and heard the testimonies of dying believers who expressed their faith in a living Savior and eternal life. How can this be? How can people who live in dying bodies talk confidently about life to other human beings who also live in fragile human bodies? Paul wrote often about this, having his mind on the heavenly realities. But that doesn't come naturally to any of us. We admit we need to learn from Paul.

In 2 Corinthians 4:13, Paul shared what he learned from the Old Testament writers.

1. What circumstances did the psalmist describe in Psalm 116:3?


2. What did the psalmist believe or acknowledge about God in Psalm 116:3–9?


3. What thoughts did the psalmist express to God in verse 10?


It was the psalmist's faith in God that encouraged him to pray to be spared from death. But his faith in God could also allow him to write further, "Precious in the sight of the LORD is the death of his saints" (v. 15). The psalmist was glad to be spared from death, yet he expressed confidence in the character of God and His viewpoint on death. Surely the psalmist understood how precious it will be to God when He welcomes His saints to His eternal home. But perhaps there is more than sentiment in the word "precious." Perhaps the psalmist understood that God recognizes how costly death is to His saints. God knows that death is an enemy that plagues all humanity, and He knows it plagues His saints as well. And the psalmist rejoiced that he had been spared in that instance.

We, too, can pray to avoid death in various circumstances. On the other hand, we can be comforted by this fact: when we have to face death in our families or among our loved ones, God knows what death costs us; He knows the high toll it demands from our lives and our emotions. Remember how Jesus wept when He saw how His friends grieved over the death of Lazarus. Remember His agony in the Garden of Gethsemane. Jesus suffered death and separation from His Father for us so that we could have life and never be separated from God. We can trust this kind of Savior.

## WORK OUT

### Inner Confidence

Introducing the picture of a tent in 2 Corinthians 5:1, Paul emphasized the *brevity* of life. It is commonly known that our bodies begin to die from birth. In 2 Corinthians 4, Paul went beyond the distresses of life to talk about the obvious end of living in a frail body—our physical death. As much as we try to put this thought out of our minds, we can never escape it. Yet for a believer, death can become the ultimate testimony of faith.

**Read 2 Corinthians 4:13–18.**

  1. Prayer is one way we can express our faith. According to 2 Corinthians 4:13, what did this spirit of faith enable Paul to do?

That is why in 2 Corinthians 4 Paul said that he had the same spirit of faith as the psalmist.

  2. Like the psalmist's faith, Paul's faith was based on something he knew about God. What did Paul know, according to 2 Corinthians 4:14?

Paul had reminded the Corinthians about this hope in 1 Corinthians 6:14, when he said that God the Father will raise believers' bodies just as He raised Jesus' body.

    3. What do 1 Thessalonians 4:16 and 17 teach about death?


    4. What does 2 Corinthians 4:14 teach about death?


First Thessalonians was one of the early books Paul wrote. At that time, he thought he might be alive when Jesus returned. He wrote, "We which are alive and remain . . . shall not prevent them which are asleep" (4:15). By the time he wrote 2 Corinthians, four or five years later, Paul had suffered many near-death experiences. He seemed to think he might be one of the dead whom Jesus would raise ("shall raise up us also," 4:14), and he was confident that he will be presented in Heaven with the Corinthians. Paul wanted Christians to look for the "uppertaker," not the undertaker.

Paul could speak confidently about the future of his body, because he knew that God will someday raise his body. That knowledge dispelled the fear of death for Paul. He believed and, therefore, spoke. Perhaps one of the reasons we cannot speak confidently to offer hope to dying people is that we sense our own lack of faith. We doubt; therefore, we cannot speak. When we believe, we can speak confidently.

    5. According to 2 Corinthians 4:15 and 16, how did Paul feel about
       ministry and the hardships he had experienced (compare with
       verses 8 and 9) for the Corinthians and others?


## Inner Renewal

From talking about the glorious, sure hope for believers' bodies in the future, Paul returned to writing about the realism of their earthly bodies. He admitted that his outward man was perishing.

    6. What truth encouraged Paul, according to 2 Corinthians 4:16?

7. According to this verse, how is a believer's inner man renewed day by day?

8. How would Psalm 1:1 and 2 help believers be renewed day by day?

9. Compare 2 Corinthians 4:16 to Romans 12:2.

## PULSE CHECK

Psalm 90:12 says, "So teach us to number our days, that we may apply our hearts unto wisdom." How realistically are you living in light of the fact that all of us will face either death or the Rapture at any moment? How are you renewing your inner man?

10. How did Paul refer to the time and weight of believers' current physical circumstances in contrast to the time and weight of their future circumstances (2 Corinthians 4:17)?

11. To keep physical problems in perspective, where should believers be looking, according to 2 Corinthians 4:18?

Compare Paul's outlook with the outlook of believers in the Old Testament, as expressed by the writer of Hebrews 11:1 and 2: "Now faith is the substance of things hoped for, the evidence of things not seen. For by it the elders obtained a good report." With these verses we come full circle to faith again. Noah was warned of things "not seen as yet" (Hebrews 11:7); Abraham "went out, not knowing whither he went" (Hebrews 11:8); others had seen promises "afar off" (Hebrews 11:13). Like these Old Testament believers, Paul looked at the "things not seen."

## Imperishable Future
**Read 2 Corinthians 5:1–8.**

In 2 Corinthians 5:1, Paul described two different kinds of body "houses"—one temporary and one permanent.

12. How does a tabernacle or tent show the temporary or fragile character of the human body?

13. What was Paul so sure about in 2 Corinthians 5:1?

Did you notice that God has something a lot more durable than a tent in the heavens waiting for believers? A building is a permanent structure. Think of the difference between the tent in the wilderness and the temple that Solomon built. The temple was far more beautiful and durable.

14. According to 2 Corinthians 5:2–4, why do believers groan in the physical body?

All of creation groans with us, according to Romans 8:22 and 23. These verses also say that our bodies groan, eagerly waiting for the adoption, or redemption, of our bodies.

15. Notice again God's wonderful plan and promise in 2 Corinthians 5:5. What is the promise, and Who is the guarantee?

As Jesus explained to Nicodemus in John 3:6 and 7, "That which is born of the flesh is flesh; and that which is born of the Spirit is spirit." Jesus declared, "Ye must be born again." Because the Spirit comes to dwell within believers, He is the guarantee of our salvation.

16. Look back to 2 Corinthians 1:21 and 22. In these verses, how did Paul describe the Spirit's work?

17. In 2 Corinthians 5:6–8, how did Paul express his confidence?

Paul had a spirit of faith that caused him to speak what he believed, as he mentioned in 2 Corinthians 4:13. Isn't that what we Christians do when we believe what the Bible says about the future and we share it with others?

## Useful Service
### Read 2 Corinthians 5:9–21.

In spite of Paul's confidence in the next life, he did not become so enamored with Heaven that he neglected the responsibilities God gave him on earth. In fact, being truly "heavenly minded" will keep a believer living effectively on earth, for God's glory and mankind's good.

18. From 2 Corinthians 5:9, what was Paul's goal, and what kept Paul on track in this life?


19. On what basis will believers be judged at the Judgment Seat of Christ, according to 2 Corinthians 5:10?


We have come full circle. Even in Heaven, what we did in our bodies will be important. As the womb is preparation for our bodies here on earth, so our time on earth is preparation for our time in eternity. Our bodies may be frail and fragile, but God has a plan and a purpose for them. In fact, He holds us accountable for what we do in our bodies.

20. Based on how much Christ loves us, what challenge did Paul give believers for noble, purposeful living (2 Corinthians 5:14, 15)?


## WEIGH IN

1. What are you currently doing to renew your inner man? Decide on a specific plan of action. Write it down so you will be more likely to follow it.


2. Admit the frail, temporary nature of your physical body. Tell God how you feel about the thought of growing older or dying. Ask Him for help to trust Him.

3. Read 1 Peter 1:22–25 to see how Peter pictured the frailty of our bodies. Because of this frailty, he urged believers to "love one another with a pure heart fervently." Now is our opportunity. Meditate on these verses and think of someone you need to love more fervently.

Does God like death and dying? No! That is why Christ came to the cross and rose victoriously. The death of a believer is precious in God's sight (Psalm 116:15). Does God enjoy seeing His people affected by the enemy of our bodies? No! But He does get glory when believing people commit their bodies and physical welfare to Him.

### Notes

1. Dr. Charles Dolph, "Thank God for Aging," *Torch* (Spring–Summer 2007), 12.

2. Ibid.

# My Body, His Temple

*"What? know ye not that your body is the temple of the Holy Ghost which is in you, which ye have of God, and ye are not your own? For ye are bought with a price: therefore glorify God in your body, and in your spirit, which are God's"* (1 Corinthians 6:19, 20).

## FITNESS GOAL

I will choose to use my sexuality to glorify God. *Does the way I think about sex glorify God? Do my actions pertaining to sex glorify God?*

We began these lessons saying that Satan desires to destroy our bodies. Sexuality is perhaps the area where Satan has his tightest hold. Television, videos, magazines, billboards—all portray women as sex objects. Women have compounded this problem because, while they often strive to be liberated from the bonds of male domination, they still try to make their bodies as attractive as possible to a crowd of male observers. Though women claim they do not want to be seen as sex objects, they still strive to be sexually appealing. Each woman needs to understand that even her sexuality can honor God, if she uses it to bring glory to Him and not to herself.

## WARM UP

Write out 1 Corinthians 6:19 and 20 and begin committing them to memory.

1. What beautiful word picture did Paul use in 1 Corinthians 6:19 to describe believers' bodies?

2. Read 1 Kings 6:18–22, 8:10 and 11, and 2 Chronicles 3:6–10 for details about Solomon's temple. Describe some special features of Solomon's temple.

3. What do 1 Corinthians 3:16 and 17 teach about the temple of God?

## WORK OUT

### A Case for Purity and Passion

Our memory verses are found between two important chapters in Scripture that deal with the body. Chapter divisions were not part of the original text, so the end of a chapter does not always end a topic of discussion. We get a sense of this when we notice the repetition of words in 1 Corinthians 6:12–20 and 7:1–5.

### Read 1 Corinthians 6:12—7:5.

1. How many times does the word "body" or "bodies" occur in 1 Corinthians 6:12—7:5?

Since the words "body" and "bodies" are repeated in both passages, it seems fitting that 1 Corinthians 6:20 forms a hinge between them. We will look at two sides of the discussion about our bodies, presented in these two sections. In chapter 6 (vv. 12–20), Paul expressed concern that all the Corinthian believers avoid sexual immorality. Any sexual fulfillment outside marriage is sexual immorality. The words "glorify God in your body" in 1 Corinthians 6:20 summarize verses 12–19 and tie them in to the first five verses of chapter 7. There Paul continued the discussion of the body and its struggle with sexual immorality, but he also addressed married people. He described the ideal of sexual passion within the marriage relationship. One thing is clear from both sides, whether you are single or married: sexual immorality is sin. Instead, God expects you to glorify Him in your body. Your body/temple is to be holy so that you can glorify God.

**"Glorify God in your body."**

The words "purity" and "passion" also summarize the set of verses on each side of this fulcrum, or hinge.

1 Corinthians 6:12–20                              1 Corinthians 7:1–5

First Corinthians 6:12–20 argues for sexual purity for all people, single or married, which is maintained by controlling passion. First Corinthians 7:1–5 then tells married people that they can have purity and avoid sexual immorality by maintaining sexual passion inside their marriage.

## PULSE CHECK

How do you feel about your sexuality? Have you thought about the fact that God cares about this intimate area of your life? He does! Have you thought about glorifying God in this most intimate area of your life? You can!

### A Case for the Body's Value

After discussing in 1 Corinthians 6:9–11 the ungodly lifestyle from which some Corinthian believers had been set free, Paul discussed the reason behind abstaining from some questionable practices.

2. In 1 Corinthians 6:12, Paul noted that although some things may be lawful, there are two important considerations. What are they?

It is human nature to look for an excuse for wrong behavior. The people of Corinth followed a common philosophy of their day to excuse their overindulgence in sex and food. This philosophy taught that the body is bad, while the spirit is good. This teaching allowed them to blame bad behavior on their evil bodies. It also allowed people to distance themselves, or their spirits, from their bodies. They claimed that only what they did in the spirit mattered and that what they did in the body did not. Based on this thinking, a person could believe that what she did with her body did not affect her thought-life, her real values, or her inner person.

People struggle with a similar philosophy today. Some people divorce themselves from responsibility for their bodies. They may hold offices of responsibility or leadership, yet they believe that their sexual impropriety has nothing to do with their integrity. Sad to say, even some Christian leaders get involved in sexual sin and somehow feel no less capable of doing their jobs.

    3. How does 1 Corinthians 6:19 and 20 address this issue?


    4. What negative and positive statements did Paul make about the body in 1 Corinthians 6:13?
       Negative


       Positive


Other people in the Corinthians' day followed a different philosophy. These people decided that since the body is bad, they should deny the body—deny its desires for food, sex, and so forth.

Some women today deny their bodies the necessary nourishment from food, causing problems like anorexia and bulimia. These women are uncomfortable with their bodies. They see their bodies as something bad or, at the least, not good.

Paul said that these philosophies were wrong, because their basic premise—that the body is bad—was wrong. The body is not bad. And for the believer, the body is for the Lord. Beginning in verse 14, Paul showed that the body is important and valuable to the Lord—in fact, to all three Persons in the Trinity.

    5. What proof is there that God the Father values believers' physical bodies (v. 14)?

6. How do we know that God the Son values our bodies (v. 15)?

7. What value does the Holy Spirit place on our bodies (v. 19)?

Paul concluded that since all three Persons of the Trinity value the believer's physical body, and since sexual immorality is a sin against the body, the believer cannot afford to dismiss what he or she does in or with the body as unimportant.

8. Look up Genesis 2:24. Why is the sin of immorality so significant, considering the fact that we are members of Christ?

9. a. According to 1 Corinthians 6:18, why is God so concerned about the particular sin of sexual immorality?

b. How does this show that He values the body?

10. Read 1 Corinthians 6:19 and 20. Record what each verse says about ownership of the believer's body.
Verse 19

Verse 20

11. a. In 1 Peter 1:17–19, what did Peter say about the price paid for the believer's body?

b. What were the details of this price?

c. What did this say about value?

12. a. According to 1 Corinthians 6:18, how should a person respond
to sexual temptation?

b. Describe some practical ways to do this.

13. How did Joseph exemplify the correct response to sexual temptation (Genesis 39:1–12)?

Paul concluded that believers must live this way—avoiding any sexual
impurity—if they want to glorify God in their bodies.

## A Case for Marital Unity
From discussing believers in general, Paul moved to discussing husbands and wives.

### Read 1 Corinthians 7:2–5.
14. Even though Paul defended the single lifestyle (1 Corinthians
7:6–8), what reason for marrying did he give in 1 Corinthians 7:2?

15. What words in 1 Corinthians 7:2–5 indicate that he was talking
about the sexual relationship in marriage?

16. What word repeated in 1 Corinthians 7:3 and 4 shows that the
husband and wife have a *mutual responsibility* in the sexual
relationship?

17. How does the wording of 1 Corinthians 7:3 show that both the
husband and the wife should gain *mutual satisfaction* from the
sexual relationship?

18. How does 1 Corinthians 7:4 support the concept of *mutual submission* in the sexual relationship and how might this impact a marriage?

If the relationship is mutual, neither one will be the loser. Each will be learning more ways to satisfy the other. And each will take his or her turn in submitting to the other. But these verses must work together. Mutual responsibility is the key. This mutually satisfying physical relationship must be a lifetime goal for couples in marriage. A beautiful balance is the key to passion that glorifies God in the sexual relationship of husband and wife.

19. What does the wording in verse 1 Corinthians 7:5 imply?

20. How could Satan tempt the partner who is deprived (1 Corinthians 7:5)?

Verse 5 makes a case for *mutual sanctification*. As each partner communicates and works toward mutual satisfaction and mutual submission, he or she helps to defeat Satan's attempts to tempt the other partner to sin. No partner can blame the other for his or her sexual sin. The Bible is clear that each person is responsible for his or her own actions. However, each partner in the marriage can help to keep the other one holy by doing his or her part in this intimate arena. And by doing so, each partner glorifies God in his or her body.

The next time you snuggle up to your husband, remember you do more than satisfy your desires or his: you glorify God in your body. Ask God for His blessing. Since purity outside the marriage arena and passion within marriage are a way to "glorify God in your body," don't be afraid to ask God for His help. He cares. It's His idea!

If you are single, divorced, or widowed, guard your purity. Evaluate and monitor your attitude. If you feel cheated by God and don't deal with it, you open yourself to temptation and a fall. Rejoice that you are the Holy Spirit's temple and focus on the joy of presenting a pure body to God.

Whether married or not, you can honor God with your sexuality.

## WEIGH IN

1. Where are you in relation to sexual purity?

Pure ——————————————————————— Impure

2. If you are single, are you keeping yourself sexually pure as a way to glorify God? If not, will you confess your sin and ask our holy God to make you holy?
3. If you are married, are you finding your sole sexual satisfaction in your partner? If not, will you ask the Lord to show you how to work on developing a sexually satisfying relationship with your husband to glorify the One Whose temple you are?

# My Body, His Priority

*"But rather seek ye the kingdom of God; and all these things
shall be added unto you. . . . For where your treasure is,
there will your heart be also" (Luke 12:31, 34).*

## FITNESS GOAL
I will measure, balance, and adjust my material needs
and wants in light of God's eternal purposes.

It's a good thing that most women like to shop! After all, a woman usually has responsibility not only for her own body, but often for the care
of her family's bodies as well. She is often the principal cook and out-
fitter; she does most of the shopping for groceries, clothes, and other neces-
sities. A lot of people joke about sales and women's interest in shopping,
but a woman is most often the one responsible to make sure the money
stretches to meet her family's needs. She is also the one who must decide
between style and cost or needs and preferences for each of the different
personalities in her family.

This may seem an easy task, but it can actually be a heavy responsibility, especially when women's magazines and advertising highlight people's
needs and seek to influence their wants. Certainly a woman cannot escape
the necessity of thinking about the temporal needs of the body.

## WARM UP
Write out Luke 12:31 and 34 and begin to memorize
them.

The Proverbs 31 woman may help us to put bodily needs into perspective. At least we can sense her involvement in these bodily needs.

1. Answer the questions (on the left) in the "My List" column. Then read Proverbs 31:10–31 and, using the right column, write how the Proverbs 31 woman might have answered the same questions.

| | My List | Her List |
|---|---|---|
| How much time do you spend shopping? | | |
| What are your main concerns when you shop for food? | | |
| What are your concerns when you shop for clothing? | | |

2. When you are planning meals, finding new recipes, and reading about the next diet, food can become a high priority. When do legitimate needs turn into worry?

3. In what way is it true that individuals who struggle with bulimia or anorexia are worrying about food?

4. a. How do you respond to the pressures of clothing style, hairstyle, and the like?

   b. Should a Christian woman ignore fashion and design, or should she strive to stay current?

5. How do you respond to this statement? "Our bodies are like magnets; they have a natural attraction for temporal things and, thus, can distract our minds from eternal realities."

## WORK OUT

## Eye Problems

Christ Himself, Who accepted the challenge of living in a human body, spoke about how to live in our own human bodies.

### Read Matthew 6:19–34 and Luke 12:1–34.

Compare the Matthew and Luke passages. Observe which statements or themes are included in both passages. Notice which statements are included only in Matthew or only in Luke.

In the first couple of verses, Matthew 6:19 and 20, Jesus contrasted treasures on earth with treasures in Heaven.

    1. What is the physical problem with treasures on earth? Check Matthew 6:19 and 20 for any additional information.

    2. What is the spiritual problem with treasures on earth? See Matthew 6:21 and Luke 12:34.

Another problem that people seem to have with treasure is that they want too much. Their eyes seem to get them into trouble because they want everything they see. The eye is one gate to the body. The eye influences our goals in life and the kind of treasure we seek.

    3. How does the eye affect the body, according to Matthew 6:22 and 23 and Luke 11:34–36?

    4. Read Proverbs 28:22 to understand the problem of an evil eye.
       a. What does a person with an evil eye do?

       b. What do Proverbs 23:6 and 7 say about an evil eye. Note: One who has an evil eye can also be called a miser, or described as "stingy."

5. According to Matthew 5:14–16, what is the purpose of a lamp?

6. a. Read Luke 11:33–36. What can cause a person's lamp to become dark?

   b. What problems could follow?

7. Luke 12:16–21 shares a parable that highlights another problem with treasure on earth.
   a. Summarize the story in one sentence.

   b. What problem did the rich farmer have?

   c. What problem regarding treasure on earth does this story highlight?

8. In Matthew 6:24, Jesus painted another word picture of treasure. What strong warning did He give about whom we serve?

In Matthew 6:22–24, Jesus seemed to present one side of the problem with treasure. My husband says it like this: "People can want too much." Yearning for earthly treasure can blind people's heavenly vision and capture their hearts. In the next verses in the passage, Jesus warned people about the other side of the problem: People can worry about not having enough. So having treasure in the wrong place is not just a problem for the rich; it can affect the poor. The evil eye can occur equally among the rich and the poor, among the "haves" and the "have-nots."

**PULSE CHECK**
Where would you place your own feelings?

I want too much.                                        I worry about not
                                                        having enough.

## Worry Problems

9. A woman's worries usually indicate what her heart really treasures or seeks after. What three worries about the body did Jesus mention in Matthew 6:25–28?

10. What value did Jesus give to the body (v. 25)?

11. From Matthew 6:26 (cf. Luke 12:24) what does Jesus want believers to learn from the birds?

12. In Matthew 6:27 and Luke 12:25 Jesus asked a rhetorical question. What point was He making about height?

13. What comparisons to lilies did Jesus make in Matthew 6:28 and 29 and Luke 12:27?

14. In Matthew 6:30 and 31 and Luke 12:28, what does Jesus want believers to learn from the grass of the field?

Notice that Jesus did not say that God does not care about our food, stature, or dress; He just doesn't want us to *worry* about any of these. In fact, God does a great job of caring for the birds and beautifying the lilies of the valley. Who can compare to His "style"?

15. What two double "ee" words are in both Matthew 6:32 and Luke 12:30? __ee__ and __ee__

16. From Matthew 6:27–32, what kinds of things do people seek?

17. In His summary, what did Jesus tell people they should seek (Matthew 6:33)?

Since people are not birds or lilies, God gives them some freedom of choice in dressing and feeding themselves. Even this part of human responsibility concerns Him enough that He will take care of it if people put first things first. The emphasis we put on our bodies—our actions, our plans, our speech, our concerns, and perhaps even our wardrobes—can show what comes first: our personal plan or His will for our lives.

18. a. What did Jesus say in Matthew 6:8 and 32 about needs?

b. If this is true, how should you respond?

If clothing or an emphasis on our bodies can influence the cause of Christ, wouldn't this be a spiritual concern? In terms of fashion, finding the line between conforming to the world and maintaining a testimony before the world can be a difficult challenge. Someone has said, "What you do speaks so loud I can't hear what you say." If this description can be applied to what we believers wear or how we take care of our bodies, then you can be sure God will direct you as you truly seek His kingdom first.

19. What might you do to put God's concerns first in the areas of clothing and fashion? Notice how Jesus taught His disciples to pray in verses 10–13 of Matthew 6.

## Greed Problems

The apostle Paul discussed the balance between "seek" and "need" in his first letter to Timothy (1 Timothy 6:6–11, 17–19). A preacher friend of mine summarized these verses this way: "Money should be a tool, not a target," something you use for God, not something you seek or strive to have just for itself.

**Read 1 Timothy 6:6–19.**

20. How might seeking first the kingdom of God relate to godliness? See 1 Timothy 6:6–8.

21. What kinds of problems did Paul warn about for those who seek or desire to be rich? See 1 Timothy 6:9 and 10.

22. How should the man or woman of God respond to the temptation for riches? See the first part of 1 Timothy 6:11.

23. What happens if you have money? If God has blessed you with riches, how should you feel or what should you do? See 1 Timothy 6:17–19.

24. What happens when you share the riches God gives you? See 1 Timothy 6:19.

## WEIGH IN

1. How much time do you give to the particular worries that Jesus highlighted? Do concerns about weight, figure, clothes, and appearance fit into these concerns?

2. Preoccupation with our bodies can send a certain message; on the other hand, carelessness about our bodies can communicate a different message. Which might be your tendency?

3. Where is the bulk of your treasure? Analyze your budget. How do you use your treasure? What we believers spend our money on or the projects we give money to are good indicators of the direction our hearts are bent.

4. What habits could you change, or what attitudes could you watch for, to help you seek the kingdom of God rather than the interests of this temporal body?

5. Pray, "Lord, make me aware of the things I seek and the things I worry about. Help me to turn these things over to You and spend my energies seeking Your will on earth. Help me to desire to be rich toward You, rather than rich toward things."

# My Body, His Tool

*"I beseech you therefore, brethren, by the mercies of God, that ye present your bodies a living sacrifice, holy, acceptable unto God, which is your reasonable service. And be not conformed to this world: but be ye transformed by the renewing of your mind, that ye may prove what is that good, and acceptable, and perfect, will of God" (Romans 12:1, 2).*

## FITNESS GOAL

I will present my body to God and let Him use my gifts for the Body of Christ. *What are my gifts? Am I using them in my church? Am I willing to use them as God leads?*

Have you ever calculated how much time you spend just trying to preserve your body? People have to spend a certain amount of time feeding their bodies, preparing the food, sitting down to eat it—not to mention the time spent shopping for the food. Think of fitness. Some people have exercise routines. They may spend twenty minutes to an hour a day walking, running, or doing aerobics. If they are ill, they spend even more time in doctors' offices or hospitals. Are you tired already? It takes a lot of time just to stay alive. Since God gave us these bodies, it is important to do what we can to care for them and preserve them.

But preservation alone should not be our focus. A friend, Pam Goller, tells the story of receiving some of her father's tools when he could no longer do the woodworking that he loved. Pam decided to preserve the tools in her collection—a level, a plane, and a square—by displaying them in a special shadow box. However, since the tools were dirty, nicked, and bent, she decided to wash and polish them for her display.

In the process, she washed off the markings on the level. It could never be used again. She had preserved it, but she had ruined any chance that it could be used again. This paints a beautiful picture of what we can do with our bodies. They will get scratched, dented, and dirty, but they will be of benefit to others. As Pam explains, "We can actually polish God's image in us by allowing ourselves to be dented and scratched. We develop a patina, a new kind of shine made because of wear and tear."

## WARM UP
Write out Romans 12:1 and 2 and begin committing them to memory.

For the next couple days, list the things you do to preserve your own body and how much time you spend on each task. Also, list things you do for other people (your family or others) and note how you feel about these tasks.

## WORK OUT
### A Dedicated Tool
Sleeping, eating, drinking, and exercising have to do with preserving our bodies. They are a natural evidence of physical life. But in Romans 12:1, Paul reminded us to "present your bodies a living sacrifice." His words turn our attention from *preservation* to challenge us to *presentation*. I heard Warren Wiersbe say, "Self-preservation is the first sign of physical life, . . . while self-sacrifice is the first sign of spiritual life."

**Read Romans 12:1.**

    1. According to Romans 12:1, what did Paul "beseech," or beg, believers to do with their bodies? Be sure to include "to" or "for whom" in your answer.

    2. a. At the end of verse 1, what reason did Paul give for believers to present their bodies to God?

b. Do you agree with Paul? Explain your answer.

3. In light of most of the Old Testament sacrifices, what is unusual about a living sacrifice? (See Leviticus 1 if you are unfamiliar with Old Testament sacrifices.)

Occasionally people present their bodies to God at the same time they receive Christ as Savior, but more often, this is a decision believers make at some later time as they grow in the Lord. But it is a definite decision, just as salvation is.

Jerry Bridges, in his book *The Discipline of Grace,* describes this step of faith as "a decisive, once-for-all dedication or commitment. We are to put our bodies at God's disposal with the same finality that an Israelite would bring his animal sacrifice to the Temple to be slain and offered up to God. At the same time, it is to be a living sacrifice, signifying a constant dedication or a perpetual sacrifice never to be neglected or recalled."[1]

4. What other words in Romans 12:1 describe the kind of sacrifice our bodies should be?

5. What alternative, given in Romans 6:11–16, did Paul want believers to avoid?

### PULSE CHECK
Stand in front of a full-length mirror and recite Romans 12:1 aloud. Have you ever specifically presented your body to God? Perhaps you should do that right now, or perhaps you need to ask God to help you come to the point where you are willing to make this commitment.

## A Renewed Tool
Perhaps you are feeling sad because you know that you cannot present

a body that is clean and holy to God. If you are willing to confess and forsake the sin that keeps you from being pure, you can still be a useful tool for God. That's what the "mercies" of Romans 12:1 are for. In God's mercy, Jesus died on the cross, took our sin upon Himself, and is willing and able to take our unholy bodies, cleanse them, and make them holy for His use.

    6. a. After you present your body to God, what else does God desire, according to Romans 12:2?

    b. What is the result of this action?

    7. What three words in verse 2 describe the will of God?

    8. What practical teaching in Psalm 1:1 and 2 will help believers practice the command, "Be not conformed . . . but be ye transformed"?

Jerry Bridges points out that Paul assumed "there are only two alternatives. Our convictions and values will come from society around us, the world, or they will come as our minds are renewed by the Word of God."[2] Paul implied that renewing our minds must be a continual process, which is why the psalmist encouraged meditating on it day and night.

## PULSE CHECK
### *Sinful society ————————— Word of God*

If your life were a continuum between sinful society and the Word of God, on which end of this continuum do you linger? How much time does it take in the Word to counter the worldly influences that bombard you daily?

Our minds are not empty vacuums; they are more like vacuum cleaners. They will suck up whatever they come into contact with—either the advice and philosophies of the world, or the admonitions and principles from the Word of God. The more we accept the influence of one, the less the other influences us. We can decide whether we will be shaped by the world or shaped by the Word.

## A Serving Tool

Often people learn Romans 12:1 and 2 as a separate entity, since its wonderful admonition stands alone so well. However, the admonition to present our bodies and renew our minds leads into the truths that Paul presented in the verses that follow. Verse 3 and following discuss specific ways that our thinking should be different.

**Read Romans 12:3–8.**

9. a. According to Romans 12:3, how should we think about ourselves?

b. How does Romans 12:16 reinforce this thought?

10. What is special about the gifts, mentioned in Romans 12:6, that God gives believers?

A renewed mind is a balanced mind. It doesn't compare itself to others. It will not think more highly of itself than it ought to, nor too lowly. But isn't it hard to be balanced? Do you ever find yourself on different days, perhaps on the same day, waffling between these extremes: either thinking that you are better than someone else, or thinking that you aren't as good as someone else, or maybe thinking that you aren't worth anything? Remembering that your body belongs to God and renewing your mind can help balance your thinking about yourself.

When we believers realize that all we have—our skills, talents, abilities, and bodies—is from God, we will be thankful. We should want to use all we have as God intended: to serve other believers in the Body of Christ. In 1 Corinthians 12:12–26 Paul compared believers to body parts with different functions, saying that some of us may be like hands or feet, but that all are essential parts of the body.

This way of thinking about our talents is different from the world's way. Before we are saved, we tend to compare ourselves with other people, rating ourselves either better or worse than they. But a transformed mind rejects this kind of thinking. God wants us to think of skills in relation to other people whom He wants us to serve. Our talents were given to us with purpose, but not for glorifying ourselves or making ourselves look good. No wonder Paul said our thinking should be transformed.

A transformed mind will immediately associate gifts with service. According to Romans 12, the main reason for presenting our bodies to God is that we might serve others in the Body of Christ with any gifts or abilities God has given to us.

We can come up with a variety of excuses for not using a gift. However, failure to use our gifts because we think we have nothing of any value to offer could stem from a form of pride. This kind of pride might reason: "Since my gift is not as great or important as another's, I can't do anything." But this "humble-sounding" thinking might stem from a desire to have something more recognizable, more prominent.

Some of us *pride* ourselves on what we can do, while others of us let *pride* keep us from trying something hard or new or menial or trivial (in our opinion). In both cases, we are really comparing ourselves as better or worse; whereas, God in effect says, "Do the best you can with the ability, or 'measure of faith' (v. 3), that I have given you. That's all that I require—that's faithfulness."

11. a. Summarize what Paul said in 1 Corinthians 4:6 and 7.


b. How do those verses help us believers renew our minds and think straight about ourselves and one another?


In Romans 12:4 and 5, Paul began to compare our physical bodies to another kind of body. In verse 4 he said that we *have* "many members in one body"; and in verse 5 he said believers *are* members of one body.

12. From Romans 12:4 and 5, explain the analogy Paul used between our bodies and the Body of Christ.

13. What statements did Paul make about the Body of Christ in Romans 12:5?

In Romans 12:1–4, Paul talked about the physical body, but in verse 5, he began to talk about a body represented by a group of people. Each believer is a member of this "one body in Christ." This is something different from the earthly physical body that Christ received when He was born of Mary. This is a brand new "Body" that consists of many saved people.

We spend a lot of time caring for our physical bodies. Paul wanted us as believers to begin to see how we are supposed to care for this new "Body in Christ," this Body of believers.

Three other passages discuss gifts and members in the Body of Christ. Each of the four passages has a slightly different emphasis. Romans 12 emphasizes using our gifts to help or edify the Body of Christ. First Peter 4 emphasizes using our gifts to glorify God. First Corinthians 12 emphasizes the unity of the Body even with its diversity. And Ephesians 4:7–16 emphasizes the specific ways that the gifts benefit the Body as a whole.

14. How do 1 Corinthians 12:20 and 27 reinforce Romans 12:5?

15. What does 1 Peter 4:8–11 teach about believers' gifts?

## A Useful Tool

The rest of Romans 12, verses 9–21, describes how a Christian should use his or her gifts. These verses actually list actions that a body presented to the Lord will do and attitudes that a transformed mind will have.

**Read Romans 12:9–21.**

Use the chart on the next two pages to answer questions 16 and 17.

16. In the middle column, list the new action or attitude that a believer with a transformed mind should have.

17. In the right column, write the action or attitude that a believer should *not* have. Sometimes the negative action is given

specifically in the verse, but not always. You may need to supply the
negative action.

| Verse | This Action or Attitude | Not This |
|-------|------------------------|----------|
| 9 | | |
| 9 | | |
| 10 | | |
| 10 | | |
| 10 | | |
| 11 | | |
| 12 | | |
| 12 | | |
| 12 | | |
| 13 | | |
| 13 | | |
| 14 | | |
| 15 | | |
| 15 | | |
| 16 | | |

| 16 | |
|----|---|
| 17 | |
| 18 | |
| 19 | |
| 20 | |
| 21 | |

Romans 12 talks about action and attitude: *presenting our physical bodies* and their gifts to God, Who gave them, and *renewing our minds* to make our bodies useful to other members in the Body. It takes a lot of time to maintain our physical bodies. How much time will you spend renewing your mind and serving others in the Body of Christ this week?

## WEIGH IN

1. Enjoy a light snack. Did you reach for something nutritious? As your snack habits may need to change, does your mind need to be transformed?

2. Which of your attitudes needs to be transformed? What action will you take to transform that attitude this week?

3. Will you commit to renewing your mind by regular study of the Word? Write a prayer of commitment.

4. Do you need to present your body to the Lord? If you haven't done it yet, will you do it now? Write a prayer of presentation.

5. What gift or ability do you think you have? Thank the Lord for it!
   Ask the Lord to help you use your gift(s) in the right way, with the
   right spirit, to serve other believers.

## Notes

1. Jerry Bridges, *The Discipline of Grace: God's Role and Our Role in the Pursuit of Holiness* (Colorado Springs: NavPress, 2006), 164.

2. Ibid., 163.

# My Body, His Plan

*"For we have not an high priest which cannot be touched with the feeling of our infirmities; but was in all points tempted like as we are, yet without sin" (Hebrews 4:15).*

## FITNESS GOAL

Following Christ's example, I will commit myself to the will of God when I am tempted or called upon to suffer unjustly. *How do I usually react to suffering? Am I thankful that Jesus took on flesh to suffer for me?*

The story is told of a little girl who woke at night, crying because of a terrible nightmare. Her mother tried to comfort her daughter and assured her that she did not need to be afraid, because Jesus was with her. The little girl responded in a plaintive voice, "I need someone with skin on." Many of us have felt this way. Although we cannot see Jesus today, over two thousand years ago "the Word was made flesh, and dwelt among us" (John 1:14). Out of love for us, Christ experienced the limitations of a physical body.

It is easier to face the struggles and temptations we experience in our physical bodies when we understand that Jesus also had a body and struggled in a similar way. And that is one reason Jesus came to earth and took on a physical body. He became our Someone with skin on.

## WARM UP

Write out Hebrew 4:15 and begin to memorize it.

According to Philippians 2:7, Jesus came to earth in the physical likeness of a man. Hebrews 2:11–14 states further that Jesus was willing to share our human limitations. This passage specifically mentions that He had a human body. "Forasmuch then as the children are partakers of flesh and blood, he also himself likewise took part of the same" (v. 14).

    1. What are some of the normal limitations of our physical bodies?


    2. Consider what it would be like for Jesus, God of the universe, to have these limitations imposed on Him. Record how these limitations would affect His life as He took on flesh for the first time.


## WORK OUT
## Christ's Physical Birth and Development
**Read Matthew 1:1–16 and Luke 1:34 and 35.**

Read the genealogy in Matthew 1:1–16 and note the change in wording as you approach verse 16. The King James Version and the New King James Version use the word "begat" to indicate the man who fathered the son. But whether the version uses the term "begat" or "father of," you will notice an abrupt change in the wording when the genealogy comes to Jesus.

    1. Compare Matthew 1:20 and Luke 1:34 and 35 and record who fathered Jesus.


Even though Jesus had a truly physical body, both Matthew and Luke make very clear that Jesus did not receive any male DNA from a human father. Instead, the Holy Spirit Himself impregnated Mary when He overshadowed her. Jesus then became the son of Mary and the Son of God in one being. We do not know the exact method God used, but we do know that no taint of original sin was passed along to Jesus as it has been to every other human being. The Son Who existed from eternity past (John 1:1) took on human flesh in the womb of Mary. Miracle of miracles!

    2. How does Galatians 4:4 fit with the genealogy of Jesus?

Not only did God wait for the right time in history to send His Son, but Jesus submitted Himself to the limitations of time while Mary waited the normal nine months for the Child to develop in her womb. As Luke indicated, when the days were completed, she brought forth her firstborn Son.

Does it seem a little disconcerting to think about Jesus in this way? We hold Him high because He is fully God, but we should also remember that He came very low for us to share our lowly physical state as fully man.

Since Jesus had a real physical body, He can demonstrate His concern for the limitations of our physical bodies. He valued our physical bodies and had a plan to redeem them. For this reason He shared in the human body so that He "might destroy him that had the power of death, that is, the devil; and deliver them who through fear of death were all their lifetime subject to bondage" (Hebrews 2:14b, 15).

   3. According to Luke 2:40 and 52, how did Jesus grow and develop as compared to other human beings?

   4. What example did Jesus set that could help children understand their responsibility to their parents (Luke 2:41–51)?

   5. List evidences of Jesus' humanness found in these passages.
   John 4:6

   John 4:7; 19:28

   Matthew 4:2; Mark 11:12

   Luke 8:23

## Christ's Victory over Temptation
### Read Matthew 4:11 and Genesis 3:1–6.

Since no taint of sin had been passed along to Jesus, Satan came along to try to spoil God's plan of redemption as he had spoiled Adam and Eve in the Garden.

6. Compare the details of Christ's temptation in Matthew 4:1–11 with the details given about Adam and Eve's temptation in Genesis 3:1–7.

a. How were the temptations similar?

b. With what were both Eve and Jesus tempted at the very first?

c. How were Eve's response and Jesus' response different?

7. What can you learn from Jesus about facing temptation?

In His physical body, Jesus showed His dependence on and His submission to the Word of God. Jesus was content with the will of God for Him; Eve was discontent. Because Jesus was victorious, He can help us in the temptations we face as we live in our physical bodies.

## PULSE CHECK
Do you use God's Word to help you defeat or overcome temptations when you face them?

The Word of God is the sword of the Spirit (Ephesians 6:17) that we need for our daily warfare. We dare not "leave home without it." Actually, we need it from the moment we wake in the morning and throughout all the waking moments of the night. We must know His Word. Praise the Lord that you are involving yourself in Bible study to keep learning. Never quit! As you learn His Word, the Holy Spirit will come alongside you to bring His Word to you at appropriate and important moments.

8. How do Hebrews 2:18 and 4:15 explain Jesus' ability to help?

Not only did Jesus' living in a physical body show that He can relate to our physical limitations, but His victory over temptation shows that He can help us have victory. Our Savior encourages us to run boldly to Him without fear of reprisal or shame, as a child unashamedly calls out in the night for help. Hebrews 4:15 and 16 assure us that Jesus sympathizes with our limitations and our temptations. The Word of God encourages us to "come boldly unto the throne of grace, that we may obtain mercy, and find grace to help in time of need."

     9. Besides depending on God's Word, what did Jesus depend on during His earthly experience? Note passages like Mark 1:35 and Luke 6:12.

We have Someone in Heaven Who truly understands our situation, yet Someone Who can also do something to help. When Jesus prayed, He had absolute confidence in God's Word and will. He wants us to depend on Him, and we demonstrate our dependence when we pray.

### PULSE CHECK
How often do you ask the Lord to give you victory over temptation?

## Christ's Example in Suffering and Death
Jesus made Himself truly vulnerable to even our archenemy—death. By wrapping Himself in a body, He became susceptible to death.

    10. How does Philippians 2:8 describe Christ's response to death on the cross?

    11. What abuses, recorded in Matthew 27:26–35, did Christ endure?

Hebrews 10:5–10 records Jesus' thoughts about taking on a body and dying as the sacrifice for sin. Note again that Jesus willingly offered His body for us. These verses end with three words in Hebrews 10:10 that express the effectiveness of Christ's sacrifice: "once for all." Jesus died once for *all people*, once *for all sin*, and once *for all time*. Old Testament animal sacrifices had to be offered over and over again, because no one sacrifice worked to get rid of sin "once for all." But Christ's sacrifice worked! That is why God the Father was pleased with His Son's sacrifice. Only His physical sacrifice could truly solve our sin problem. Only His blood was effective to cleanse sin.

12. What words are repeated in Hebrews 10:7 and 9 that express Christ's willingness to die as our sacrifice?

The story is told of a man who could not understand the gospel. One Sunday morning while he waited for his wife to return from church, a strong wind began to blow. It blew so hard that birds began to fly against the window. The man tried to tap on the window to shoo the birds in another direction—to no avail. Several swooped toward the window, only to fall sharply when their necks were broken by the force of the impact. "If only I could become a bird," he thought, "then I could make them understand." Then suddenly, he understood. The only way God could reach man was to become man, in the person of His Son.

Christ's death atones for our sin, which removes our guilt and punishment. If we admit that we are sinners and accept Him and His sacrificial death as the atonement for our personal sin, He saves us; He rescues us. We become His children, miraculously born again by the Holy Spirit.

13. According to 1 John 3:16 and 4:7–11, how should Christ's death affect the way we treat other people?

14. According to 1 Peter 2:19–21, what kind of suffering is commendable for a believer?

15. According to 1 Peter 2:21, how was Christ's suffering supposed to affect us?

16. How did Jesus respond to suffering, according to 1 Peter 2:23?

17. In 1 Peter 4:19, what similar way did Peter tell believers to respond to suffering?

18. According to 1 Peter 2:24, how should Christ's bearing our sins in His own body affect how we live (act and react)?

19. How does each of these verses illustrate that Christ committed Himself to God during suffering?
Matthew 26:39

Mark 14:36

Luke 22:42

Luke 23:46

You may be suffering unjustly. Living in a body opens us to real physical, emotional, or verbal pain caused by other people, as Christ knew well. You might have tried every legitimate means to defend yourself, but it only seemed to make things worse. There may be many occasions when your best response is simply to repeat the words of Jesus in Gethsemane, "Not my will, but thine, be done." As Jesus did, you can ask that a situation be removed, but peace comes when you surrender, regardless of whether the situation changes or not. When peace comes, you know God has heard your prayer—even as He heard Christ's prayer.

Some people suffer because of someone else's sin. Abuse of children and women continues to be an ongoing scourge here and abroad. Sometimes abuse is overlooked or excused by those who do the abusing. Any woman who is being abused should seek immediate help from a pastor or the police. Every kind of abuse leaves scars—in the body or the mind. But a growing relationship with the Lord Jesus can bring healing for those scars. His death not only atones for our own sin, but it gives us an example of how to respond to the sins of others. Understanding His death should encourage us to die to our own desires and to suffer criticism without fighting back. Because He died for us, we should be willing to die to self, giving up our desires and goals in order to serve others.

## WEIGH IN

If possible, meditate on your knees.

    1. a. What distressing situation are you facing today?

       b. How might the submissive words of Jesus in His hour of agony be appropriate for your situation?

    2. Ask God for wisdom to respond to unjust criticism or unjust treatment as Jesus did. It may be helpful to write out your prayer.

    3. a. What temptations are you facing right now?

       b. How can you respond as Jesus did?

    4. Write out Scripture verses that will help you deal with your temptations and suffering. Memorize them to have them at your mental fingertips.

    5. Remember to run to Jesus—even as He, when He lived on earth, went to His Father.

# My Body, His Victory

*"Jesus said unto her, I am the resurrection, and the life: he that believeth in me, though he were dead, yet shall he live: And whosoever liveth and believeth in me shall never die. Believest thou this?" (John 11:25, 26).*

## FITNESS GOAL

I will learn to live with hope and without fear of death beuse of God's promise that I will live eternally with Jesus in my glorified body. *Am I confident about where I will spend eternity? Am I sharing my hope of eternal life in Jesus with others?*

## WARM UP

Write out John 11:25 and 26 and begin committing them to memory.

Even if we use the latest antiaging creams, are faithful in our fitness routines, and eat healthy foods, our bodies will eventually wear out and die. Throughout history people have sought a fountain of youth to stave off the inevitable deterioration of their bodies. But as Ponce de León discovered, the fountain of youth is merely a figment of someone's imagination. Yet believers have a different fountain from which to draw. The psalmist declared in Psalm 36:9, "For with thee is the fountain of life." All life stems from God, physical life and eternal life. Therefore, death is not something that needs to be feared, but it is something that needs to be prepared for.

1. Record the number of deaths you hear or read about this week.

2. The Bible says the average life span is 70 years, or 25,550 days. If you live to 70, calculate approximately how many days you have left on earth (70 minus your age x 365). If you have already passed 70, how many extra days have you had (your age minus 70 x 365)?

## WORK OUT

### God's Future Plan for Changing Our Bodies
**Read 1 Corinthians 15:19–52.**

We have discussed the importance of our bodies on earth, but we must understand that even in death our bodies are important, because God has a future plan for our bodies! Since all of us are mortal flesh, it is important that we know what the Bible says about the future of our physical frame. Paul admitted in 1 Corinthians 15:19, if our hope in Christ is good only for this life, "we are of all men most miserable," because people die. This lesson helps explain what happens to the bodies of believers after they die.

1. According to Romans 8:22 and 23, we believers groan along with all of creation. But what should we, who have the firstfruits of the Spirit, be eagerly awaiting?

2. a. What promise is given in 1 Corinthians 15:20–22?

b. What is the promise based on?

Centuries ago, a farmer would call the first portion of his harvest the firstfruits. Usually the firstfruits were a guarantee that more of the harvest would soon follow. Christ was the first to be resurrected who would never die again. His resurrection, as the firstfruits of the harvest, guaranteed that we can look forward to a bodily resurrection as well.

3. a. What do 1 Corinthians 15:25 and 26 describe as the last enemy?

b. How will Christ deal with it?

4. What questions might be raised in a discussion about the redemption of our bodies?

5. How might you begin to answer question 4 after reading 1 Corinthians 15:36–44?

6. Name some things that must be changed in our bodies for them to live eternally (1 Corinthians 15:50–54).

God created us to be able to live in earth's atmosphere. We are born with bodies that breathe air. Our lungs are able to take oxygen from the air. Fish are created with gills that enable them to get oxygen out of the water; whereas, we would drown in water. Just as God created us to live on land here in our earth's atmosphere, He will have to re-create us to live in the new heaven and earth. Our new bodies will not be tainted by sin; they will not be subject to time or decay.

Instead our bodies will be like Jesus' resurrected body. He already provided us with new life when we were saved, or born again, but our earthly bodies still decay and die. However, God plans to change our bodies in such a way that they will be fit to live with Him forever. Second Corinthians 5:1 compares the physical, corruptible body to a tent that will be cast off for an incorruptible house in Heaven that is eternal.

7. Describe the events and the changes that will take place in our physical bodies, according to 1 Corinthians 15:51 and 52.

8. How long will it take for all these huge changes, according to 1 Corinthians 15:52?

9. How do 1 Corinthians 15:54 and 55 explain Christ's victory over death?

## God's Plan to Resurrect Our Bodies

10. a. What information from 1 Corinthians 15:51 and 52 is emphasized again in 1 Thessalonians 4:13–17?

b. What additional information does 1 Thessalonians 4:13–16 give to comfort those facing death?

## Read 1 Thessalonians 4:13–17.

11. Record the words that Paul used in 1 Thessalonians 4:13–16 to describe the dead.
    Verse 13

    Verse 14

    Verse 15

    Verse 16

The beauty of sleep is that you plan to wake up. Those who are "dead in Christ" will awake. That's why Jesus could tell Martha in John 11:26, "And whosoever liveth and believeth in me shall never die." Another thing we learn in 1 Thessalonians 4:13–17 about believers who die is that while their bodies go to the grave, they go to be with Christ. At the moment when the trumpet sounds, the Lord will bring those believers with Him; but at the same time, their former bodies will be raised. Thus, in an instant, those believers will be reunited with their bodies.

## PULSE CHECK
Do you have this hope of eternal life? If not, place your faith in Jesus right now.

## Christ's Resurrected Body

From the previous verses it is understood that the resurrection of Jesus

Christ is the foundation for the resurrection of believers. For this reason, it is important that each believer understand the significant facts show-ing that Christ rose bodily from the grave. The disciples themselves were unsure at first about Jesus' resurrection. After forty days and several oppor-tunities to meet and eat with their Lord, the apostles were finally convinced of Jesus' resurrection.

   12. What expression and proofs did Luke offer in Acts 1:3 and 4 to convince Theophilus that Christ had really risen from the dead?


John declared in 1 John 1:1–3 that he had heard Jesus Christ, seen Him personally, and even touched Him. Besides these eyewitness testimonies, the change in the men's personalities was another proof. Luke recorded these changes in his book of Acts.

   13. a. As you note the apostles' testimony to the Resurrection in the early chapters of Acts, what kinds of risks were the disciples taking?


      b. How did the disciples' message or actions display boldness, as recorded in the following verses:
      Acts 2:32


      Acts 3:14–26


      Acts 4:18–29


      Acts 5:29–32


The risks that the disciples were willing to take testify to the reliability of the Resurrection. The apostles tried to convince their Jewish audience that Jesus had risen from the dead. On several of these early occasions, they risked imprisonment and their lives to keep making their claim that Jesus was really alive. Before they saw Jesus alive, they were cowering together behind closed doors, but after His resurrection and the coming of the Holy Spirit, they were bold and daring in their witness.

The apostles confirmed their eyewitness accounts by using Old Testament Scriptures to assure their Jewish audiences that Jesus' death and resurrection had been foretold in their Scriptures. (Hint: We, too, should use Scripture when we witness.)

14. How did Peter use Psalm 16:8–11 and 110:1–4 in Acts 2:22–36 to affirm the resurrection of Jesus?

15. In Acts 13:33–37, how did Paul use Psalm 2:7 and 16:8–11 to affirm the resurrection of Jesus?

16. Paul often used his own testimony of salvation as proof for the resurrection. According to Acts 9:1–18, what persuaded Paul that Jesus is alive?

17. What proofs of Christ's resurrection did Paul list in 1 Corinthians 15:3–8?

## PULSE CHECK

Which of the evidences mentioned so far are the most convincing to you? Can you summarize the evidences in your own words to share with others?

## God's Future Plan to Give Us a Body like His

Another reason the resurrection of Jesus is so important to believers is that our new bodies will resemble His resurrection body.

18. What will happen to our bodies? See Philippians 3:20 and 21.


19. What can you learn about our future from 1 John 3:1–3?



After the resurrection, Jesus had a real body. He ate food, had the scars from His crucifixion, and could be touched. Yet He also could appear in a different form, enter right through a closed door, and enter Heaven through a cloud. His body had been changed and glorified. In conclusion of this study on our bodies, take a moment to consider the glory of Jesus Christ, Who will reign for all eternity in His glorified body.

## Praise and Honor to Jesus in His Glorified Body

20. In Hebrews 1:1–4 and 8:1 and 2, what descriptions did the writer of Hebrews use to portray the glory of the risen Jesus?


21. Describe the glory of Jesus that John saw and recorded in Revelation 1:12–16.



A theme of Revelation 5 is that Jesus Christ is worthy.

22. Revelation 5:1–7 explains that only Jesus is worthy to open the book of judgment. How does this passage describe His glory as well as His humanity?
Glory

Humanity

23. a. According to Revelation 5:6–9, where does the Lamb stand?

b. How is He worshiped?

If Christ has a real body—and He does—and since He will retain that body into eternity, we have another reason for realizing that our bodies have eternal significance. Like Job, we can look forward to seeing Him in His body as we stand in our bodies. Therefore, we should not denigrate or misuse them, but thank the Lord for them and use them for His glory. We should also be praising the Lord for all He has accomplished for our lowly bodies—both on earth and for eternity.

## WEIGH IN

God did not make a mistake when He made us the first time. Except for the effects of sin, we have the exact body He wants us to have. Someone might ask, "If God can prepare us with new, heavenly bodies, why would He bother to raise our old bodies?" I don't know for sure, but it seems obvious that this is further evidence that He values the human body.

For several weeks we have thought about our bodies. We wanted to see them from God's perspective, weigh our bodies according to His scale. He has a plan for our bodies; He has eternal purpose for them.

1. Have you trusted in Jesus' death and resurrection? If you have, you can sing, "Oh, that will be glory for me."

2. How might you respond to someone who said your hope in a living Savior is no better than the legend of the fountain of youth?

3. Make a list of reasons why Jesus is worthy of praise and honor, and write a prayer of worship to thank Him for each of those things.
   List

   Prayer

4. Since He is worthy, how will you use your body to glorify Him?

# LEADER'S GUIDE

## LEADER'S GUIDE

As you use this study guide, be flexible. It is simply a tool to aid in the understanding of God's Word. Adapt it to suit your unique group of women and their needs. The discussion questions are optional; the answers are provided to clarify my intent and stimulate your thought. You may have an entirely different insight as the Holy Spirit illumines your heart and mind. Each section of the study has a specific purpose.

The introductory paragraphs furnish background information and lead into the topic of that lesson.

The Fitness Goal states the learning objective, similar to an ideal weight, and synthesizes the life change that absorbing the truths of God's Word in this lesson will help each woman to achieve. These are not for discussion. But do remind the ladies to note them.

Each lesson has a "fitness routine," which includes a Warm Up and a Work Out section.

The Warm Up section includes the memory verse and "food for thought" questions. The memory verse may be the most important part of each lesson. Encourage the women to work hard to learn it so that it will become part of their "new" self. The Warm Up questions will start each woman thinking about the topic of the lesson. Answers may come from a woman's own experience or from particular Scriptures.

The Work Out section takes each one deeper into Scripture. As with any good fitness routine, it is wise to take a couple days a week for these. These questions need to be answered directly from the text that is referenced. The purpose of each question is to get to know what the Word says, rather than each one's best guesses. The questions will exercise the women's minds and stretch their spiritual muscles as they wrestle with the thoughts in each passage.

The Pulse Checks come in the middle of the Work Out sections and provide time-outs for each woman to think about what she has been learning. These questions do not require written responses and are not for discussion.

The Weigh In section is not for group discussion. However, it provides opportunity for each woman to write out an application that is personal to her. This is where each woman can measure her own spiritual progress. It is during her "weigh in" that she may want to look back to the Fitness Goal to measure her progress. Encourage the ladies to apply what they have studied.

As with any group Bible study, its effectiveness usually depends on two things: (1) the leader herself and (2) the women's commitment to prepare beforehand and interact during the study. You cannot totally control the second factor, but you have total control over the first one. The following brief suggestions will help you be an effective Bible study leader.

Prepare each lesson a week in advance. During the week, read supplemental material and look for illustrations in the everyday events of your life as well as in the lives of others.

Encourage the women in the Bible study to complete each lesson before the meeting itself. This preparation will make the discussion more interesting.

Also encourage the ladies to memorize the key verse or verses for each lesson. Allow time in class for women to recite their verse, individually or as a group, or both. (The verse is printed below the title of each lesson.) If possible, print the verses on 3 x 5 cards to distribute each week. If you cannot do this, suggest that the women make their own cards and keep them in a prominent place throughout the week. A fast way to print verses is to type them onto self-adhesive label paper, then stick each to a 3 x 5 card, which may even have the figure of a lady glued to it first.

Provide an informal, comfortable setting. A circle of chairs, chairs around a table, someone's living room or family room: all of these encourage women to relax and participate. In addition to an informal setting, create an atmosphere in which ladies feel free to participate and be themselves.

### 1½-hour Bible Study

10:00—10:30          Bible study
Leader guides discussion of half the questions in the day's lesson.

10:30—10:45          Coffee and fellowship
10:45—11:15          Bible study
Leader continues discussion of the questions in the day's lesson.

11:15—11:30          Prayer time

## ANSWERS FOR LEADER'S USE

*Information inside parentheses ( ) is for the group leader. The information might be suggestions for something to do, or it might be additional commentary to share with the group as appropriate and if time allows.*

### LESSON 1

**Warm Up**—1. (a) God reminded Belshazzar that his breath was in God's hands. God controlled Belshazzar's life and death. (b) King Belshazzar was "found wanting." That means that in God's scale of measurement, Belshazzar was underweight; he lacked what God was looking for. Belshazzar was an idolater and did not express any faith in God.

2. Answers will vary, but, for example, a picture of a shapely woman in a bathing suit implies that we all must aspire to look like her, to achieve a body shape like hers.

3. Aging can make a woman feel less capable; she may feel depressed about wrinkles, etc. Weight problems can cause a person to feel less valuable than an "ideally" shaped person. An overweight person may either refuse to eat enough to be nourished properly, or she may force herself to throw up after eating.

4. In the image of God, since both male and female are included in "let us make man in our image. . . . Male and female created He them."

**Work Out**—1. "What is man that you are mindful of him?" (v. 4). "Thou . . . hast crowned him with glory and honour" (v. 5). "Thou madest him to have dominion over the works of thy hands" (v. 6). David couldn't help but end the psalm by giving God the glory: "O LORD our Lord, how excellent is thy name in all the earth!" (v. 9).

2. In Colossians 2:9 the word "Godhead" is used to imply more than one Person, yet the One Person referred to, Jesus, embodies all the qualities of the whole.

3. *Genesis 1:2*—God the Holy Spirit. *Genesis 2:7*—God the Holy Spirit. *Exodus 20:11*—God the Father. (The average Jewish reader would understand this to be the Father.) *Job 33:4*—God the Holy Spirit. *John 1:2*—God the Son. *Hebrews 1:8–10*—God the Son. (It is difficult to separate their individual contributions, since they are One, but these verses should make it clear that all the Persons of the Godhead were involved in Creation.)

4. It was good, very good, including the human body.

5. He questioned God's word.

6. The fruit would have been tempting to the senses of Eve's body: sight, smell, taste, and maybe even touch.

7. The woman would have pain in childbirth; the man would sweat and find work difficult. Both of their bodies would return to dust.

8. Adam and Eve were not ashamed of their bodies before they sinned, but they were embarrassed and wanted to cover up after their sin. They became self-conscious—a subtle problem that often becomes our enemy.

9. (a) Satan struck Job with painful boils from the sole of his feet to the top

of his head. (b) Satan thought that attacking Job's body would be the thing that would cause Job to curse God.

10. Job knew that God had fashioned him from clay and clothed him with skin and flesh, knit him with sinews and bones. Job also knew that someday God would restore his flesh so that he would see God in his flesh, even after his body had died and been destroyed by worms.

11. (a) The psalmist knew that God's hands had fashioned him and had made his inward parts while he was still in his mother's womb. He knew he was skillfully and wonderfully made. (b) Personal answers.

12. Circumcision.

13. Paul may very well have had scars from being whipped, beaten, and stoned. He referred to them as the marks of the Lord Jesus. (Paul viewed his scars as signs of God's ownership, like those put on slaves and cattle.)

14. Christ died for our sins. Other verses describe His crucifixion. Then His body was actually buried, proving He really died. Then on the third day He rose again. And other Scriptures tell us that people saw His scars.

15. God's own Son was born of a woman to redeem us and adopt us as sons. Isn't God kind! He could have bypassed the woman, but instead He used the woman.

16. The price of our redemption, or purchase price, was not paid with mere silver or gold, but with Christ's own blood.

17. Jesus bore our sins in His own body on the cross.

**Weigh In**—(Some answers are personal, but it might be uplifting if a few of the women share the verses they chose as helpful to them.)

## LESSON 2

(You may end up taking the entire study time to discuss the first six questions. Don't feel bad about this. The ladies will have learned on their own by answering the other questions, and the first Weigh In challenge may be the best application. If you have more time, decide which of the other questions might be best for your class to discuss or answer together.)

**Warm Up**—1. Answers will vary.

2.

| Reference | Name | What Else Is Noted | Who Noted It |
|---|---|---|---|
| Genesis 12:11, 14, 15 | Sarai (Sarah) | Nothing. | Abraham's servant; Abraham, the Egyptians, and the princes of Pharaoh. |
| Genesis 24:2, 11–21, 58, 64, 67 | Rebekah | Nothing. | The writer of Genesis. |
| Genesis 29:16–20 | Rachel | Her form and appearance were appealing. | Jacob. |

| Reference | Name | What Else Is Noted | Who Noted It |
|---|---|---|---|
| 1 Samuel 25:3, 32–42 | Abigail | She was also a woman of good understanding. | The writer of 1 Samuel indicates this, but David seemed to notice. |
| 2 Samuel 11:2–5 | Bathsheba | She was the wife of Uriah. | David. |
| Esther 1:11–13, 15–19 | Vashti | She was ordered to parade her beauty for a group of men. | Ahasuerus, her husband. He wanted to flaunt her beauty to glorify himself before his cohorts. |
| Esther 2:7–9, 15–17 | Esther | She was lovely and beautiful. | The king's officers. Beautiful women were considered a status symbol. |

3. *Sarai*—Sarai's beauty got her into trouble. *Rebekah*—She became Isaac's wife, mainly because of her spirit rather than her beauty. *Rachel*—Rachel's beauty (and being loved by Jacob) caused jealousy problems with her sister. *Abigail*—Her beauty didn't affect her behavior; she wasn't spoiled. It also didn't improve her husband. *Bathsheba*—Bathsheba's beauty led to David's downfall. *Vashti*—Beauty probably got her the position of queen, but then it got her into trouble, and she lost her position as queen. *Esther*—Esther's husband, King Ahasuerus, may have had selfish goals in relationship to Esther's beauty, but God overruled and used Esther to save Israel.

4. From Webster's New World Dictionary: *Beauty*—(1) the quality of being very pleasant, as in form, color, tone, behavior, etc. *Virtuous*—having, or characterized, by moral virtue (quality regarded as good).

**Work Out**—1.

| Ruth | Proverbs 31 Woman |
|---|---|
| 3:11—The town knew Ruth as virtuous. | 31:1, 10—Lemuel's mother called her virtuous. |
| 1:16; 2:12—Ruth feared the Lord. | 31:30—She feared the Lord. |
| 2:3—Ruth used her hands to work hard. | 31:13, 14—She used her hands and brought food from afar. |
| 2:11—Ruth was kind. | 31:26—She opened her mouth with kindness. |
| 2:17, 18—Ruth shared with her mother-in-law. | 31:15—She provided for her household. |
| 3:8–11—Ruth was someone Boaz could trust. | 31:11—Her husband trusted her. |

2. (a) God described His criterion as being what's inside, that is, what's in a person's heart. (b) In Proverbs 31, the woman is noted for what is on the inside, her fear of the Lord. That is lasting, compared to outward appearances, which can change.

3. Based on his outer "presence," the Corinthians judged Paul as weak and his speech as contemptible.

4. He asked who had made them differ from one another, who had given them what they had, and why they gloried in what they had received. (God makes each of us unique. Since God made us, we have no reason to boast or feel down on ourselves.)

5. The Holy Spirit comes to live inside each believer, so each is a temple for Him.

6. She strengthened her arms (v. 17), and she made beautiful clothing for herself. She wore scarlet, fine linen, and purple.

7. Naomi advised Ruth to wash and anoint herself (probably with perfumes) and put on her best garment. In other words, to dress up.

8. What you "wear" on the inside is more important to God than what you wear on the outside. He values the attitude of a meek and quiet spirit. (This doesn't necessarily refer to a woman who doesn't talk. This refers to a woman who is strong enough to give up her own way to please someone else, especially her husband. This kind of woman may be a bubbly conversationalist and outgoing, yet she may be quiet in that she is not demanding and pushy. She ultimately trusts the Lord and doesn't have to push and fuss to get her own way. She may make suggestions; but she trusts God, knowing He is the One Who is really in control.)

9. God cautioned against being with winebibbers or gluttons. That is, He warned against eating or drinking more than the body needs and becoming poor and drowsy.

10. The guideline is to give thanks to God for what you eat.

11. In 1 Timothy 4:6, Paul emphasized that it is most important to be nourished in the words of faith and good doctrine.

12. Jesus emphasized the same thing in Matthew 4:4 when he quoted the Old Testament: "Man shall not live by bread alone, but by every word that proceedeth out of the mouth of God" (cf. Deuteronomy 8:3). Jesus taught that God's Word is more important than food.

13. Possible answers include the following. *Principle:* Do not judge one another for what the other person eats, because what you eat is between you and God. *Principle:* Be considerate. Don't cause someone else to stumble. Do not grieve or destroy another person just so you can eat what you want. (Ask the ladies for examples, such as, it could mean not to eat dessert or things made with sugar if it would be tempting to your diabetic friend. It depends on the weakness or strength of your friend.) *Principle:* Do not destroy the work of God for any personal preference, whether that is for food or anything else. *Principle:* Pursue peace and edification of (building up) other believers. *Principle:* Don't encourage someone to eat or drink something she has doubts about. *Principle:* What we eat or don't eat does not commend us to God. *Principle:* Consider your sister (or brother) when you eat. If food makes your sister stumble, refrain from eating.

14. Glorify God in *everything*. (God really does care about our eating and drinking; He just doesn't measure it by calories. He wants us to care about His glory—about magnifying Him by nurturing our souls in His Word and valuing believers for whom He died.)

15. (a) Paul mentioned runners and boxers. All runners in a race run, but only one wins the prize. Boxers fight other boxers, not the air. Both discipline their bodies to compete and win a temporal prize. (b) Paul disciplined his body for the gospel's sake, to win a prize from the Lord and to avoid doing something that would hurt his testimony.

16. (a) Paul said that bodily exercise profits a little. (b) The best kind is exercise unto godliness, because it is profitable for all things. (This kind of exercise involves choices as indicated by verse 7: "Refuse profane and old wives' fables." Someone has said that the best exercise is pushing away from the table. Likewise, the best godly exercise is turning from known sin or false teaching and turning to the Scriptures for positive reinforcement.)

17. That God's beauty be seen in her, that others are attracted to the Lord, and that He makes her life and work of value and beauty to others.

**Weigh In**—(You may want to lead the women in singing "Let the Beauty of Jesus" [from question 4] if you all are familiar with the song).

## LESSON 3
**Warm Up**—1. In the absence of a synagogue in Philippi, Paul went to the river, where he found a group of women who gathered for prayer. Lydia, a seller of purple, became the first believer in Philippi. Later, Paul and Silas cast demons out of a slave girl and were jailed. The jailor and his family accepted the Lord and were baptized. Lydia is the only named believer, but her household and some of her friends, the slave girl, and the jailor's family were a few of the first believers in the church.

2. While in prison, Paul and Silas sang praises to God, and other prisoners heard them singing. They were able to share the message of salvation with the jailor and his household, who were then saved.

3. Several times the Philippians sent items to meet Paul's needs. Then the church sent Epaphroditus with supplies and as a personal comfort.

**Work Out**—1. That their love would abound in knowledge and discernment and that they would think straight, live right, and produce much.

2. Paul's chains (imprisonment) helped to spread the gospel. For example, the palace guards who were bound to him heard the gospel.

3. The believers became more confident to share the gospel in Paul's place. Even though not all of them had the right motive, Paul rejoiced that the gospel was being given out by others. (Apparently some began telling the gospel for the wrong reasons, but Paul didn't care. He was just glad that Christ was preached. He did not care who got the credit for it.)

4. Christ was preached—and Paul was thrilled!

5.

| Reference | Mention of the Gospel and Bonds | Summary |
|---|---|---|
| 1:5 | "your fellowship in the gospel" | Paul was thankful for the Philippians' fellowship in the gospel. |
| 1:7 | "both in my bonds, and in defense and confirmation of the gospel" | The Philippians shared with Paul what God was doing through him, whether he was free or in bonds. |
| 1:12 | "unto the furtherance of the gospel" | People knew that Paul was in prison because of Christ, not for breaking the law. Anyone he came into contact with heard the gospel. |
| 1:17 | "set for the defence of the gospel" | Paul was going to continue spreading the gospel even while some others thought to make matters worse for him. |
| 1:27 | "let your conversation be as it becometh the gospel of Christ" | Paul told the believers to conduct themselves in a way that was worthy of the gospel of Christ. |
| 1:27 | "with one mind striving together for the faith of the gospel" | They were to stand together as one man in contending for the truth ("the faith of the gospel"). |

6. Paul asked for more opportunities to share Christ. He did this even though he was in bonds because he had shared the gospel.

7. Paul wanted to be as bold as always, and he didn't want to do anything to shame the gospel. He wanted to make Christ look good—to magnify Him by life or by death.

8. (a) Paul's reason for living was Christ. (b) Paul knew that to die would be gain, for he would be in Heaven with Christ. So he was not afraid to die.

9. (a) Paul didn't know whether to choose life or death. Staying alive would be for the Philippians' benefit. (b) He cared about others more than he cared about himself. He wanted his life to help them progress and have joy in the Christian life.

10.

| Goals | Prayer Requests |
|---|---|
| Honor the gospel with your life (v. 27). | Increase in love, knowledge, and judgment. |
| Maintain unity (v. 27). | Approve things that are excellent. |
| Continue to strive for the faith (v. 27). | Be sincere and without offense. |
| Don't be afraid of your enemies (v. 28). | |

11. They would also be called upon to suffer.

12. Christ was willing to humble Himself, willing to limit His supernatural powers for the sake of sinners. (Ask: How could God use our experiences for the gospel's sake?)

13. By pleasing God through behavior that illustrated salvation, such as serving without murmuring, being blameless and harmless before a wicked world, being shining lights, and holding forth the Word of life.

14. *Timothy*—He was like-minded with Paul. Timothy would care for the Philippians just as Paul would. Timothy was willing to put his body through the rigors of travel from Rome to Philippi just to be an encouragement to them. *Epaphroditus*—He had put the Lord's work and his care for Paul above concern for his own body, even his health. (This was truly mutual care—the Philippians and Epaphroditus caring for Paul, Epaphroditus and Paul caring for the Philippians, and Paul and Timothy caring for the Philippians. We must exert physical energy as we meet the needs of friends or loved ones. Paul and his friends keep reminding us: do it—expend energy—for the gospel's sake.)

15. Paul wanted to gain the knowledge of Christ, of the power that had raised Christ from the dead, and of fellowship with Christ through his own suffering for Him. Paul wanted to be conformable to Christ's death.

16. They want to gain earthly things; their belly is their god. They seek to satisfy their fleshly desires. (Discuss: Do we ever blame lack of ministry on our bodies, saying that we are too tired, that we do not have the right personality or training, that we have some physical disability? Are we putting our bodies before the Lord's service?)

17. As believers, we look for the Savior from Heaven, where our citizenship is. Our limited bodies will be transformed to be like Christ's glorious body. Even the best human body is limited; it is earthly, corruptible, subject to disease and aging. We all await this glorious transformation.

**Weigh In**—(Sharing Weigh In answers should always be voluntary. But if ladies volunteer, their sharing can help your group bond. Close with prayer for any limitations/victories that were shared. Be sure to pray for yourself as well so you come across as a fellow struggler, growing with the ladies you are teaching.)


## LESSON 4

**Warm Up**—1. Personal answers; they will vary.

2. You can sometimes tell what people are thinking just by the way they act or react. It is as though they are an open book that you can read.

**Work Out**—1. (a) A reference letter is a letter written by a previous employer, teacher, coach, or someone else who can honestly speak about a person's skills and abilities. Its purpose is to make a good impression for the person being written about. (b) Personal answers.

2. Paul called them "epistles," or letters, "of commendation."

3. (a) Paul was talking about a human letter, not a paper letter. These letters

were written with the Holy Spirit rather than with ink. (b) They were written on the believers' hearts, not on tablets. He told the Corinthians, "Ye are our epistle" (v. 2) and repeated this again in verse 3: "Ye are manifestly declared to be the epistle."

4. Paul meant that the Corinthians' testimony served as a reference letter for him. The testimony of their lives could be seen, or "read," by anyone who saw them or heard of them. People could see the changes that the Holy Spirit had made in them.

5.

| Paul's Ministry | Moses' Ministry |
|---|---|
| Tablets of flesh, engraved on flesh, or the heart (3:3) | Tablets of stone, engraved on stones (3:7) |
| A new covenant (3:6) | Old [covenant] Testament (3:14) |
| Not of the letter—of the Spirit (3:6) | Of the letter (3:6) |
| Spirit gives life (3:6) | Letter kills (3:6) |
| Ministry of the Spirit | Ministry of death (3:7, 8) |
| More glorious | Glorious |
| Ministry of righteousness (3:9) | Ministry of condemnation (3:9) |
| Remains (3:11) | Passing away (3:11) |
| Paul speaks boldly about this (3:12) | Moses had his face veiled (3:13) |
| Veil taken away, when one turns to the Lord (3:16) | Veil also on people's minds and hearts, even to Paul's day (3:14, 15) |
| We all | Only Moses |
| We all with unveiled face (3:18) | Moses' face was veiled, so were the minds of his listeners (3:13–15) |
| We behold the glory of the Lord | They could not look at the glory on Moses' face (3:7) |
| We are transformed into His image as we look (3:18) | The Israelites couldn't look |
| A growing glory—we are transformed from glory to glory | A fading glory (3:7) |

6. They are blind, having been blinded by Satan.

7. A veil covered the Israelites' spiritual eyes.

8. The Holy Spirit removes the veil.

9. We behold the glory of the Lord, and we are transformed into His image as we look (3:18). Each time you get a new glimpse of Christ's glory in your study of the Word, the Spirit begins to change you into that image.

10. To obey the Word instead of ignoring what it says.

11. Mercy and truth, which involve God's laws and commandments.

12. The Spirit of the Lord, the Holy Spirit, does the changing.

13. (a) The ministry of the Spirit changed Paul's life. Paul was open, having renounced hidden (secret and shameful) things. He was bold, not crafty or presenting the Word of God deceitfully. He could commend himself before others and God. (b) Through the Spirit, Paul lived openly and honestly before people; he was content for people to "read" him and his motives. In chapter 6 he became more explicit: He said that he gave "no offence in any thing, that the ministry be not blamed" (v. 3).

**Weigh In**—(Give ladies an opportunity to pray their prayers of commitment [question 3]—if they choose. If none of them prays, simply close in prayer, perhaps praying your own words of commitment.)

## LESSON 5

**Warm Up**—1. A clay pitcher, a torch, and a trumpet.

2. To hide the light until Gideon signaled with his trumpet.

3. At Gideon's signal, each man blew his trumpet and broke his clay pitcher, allowing the lights of three hundred torches to suddenly surround the frightened Midianite army. The result was victory for the Israelites and defeat for the Midianites.

**Work Out**—1. The gospel of the glory of Christ, Who is the image of God (4:4).

2. Our bodies are perishable. They were made to be used by God. They can be filled with a treasure. They can be used even when they are broken.

3. That Christ died for our sins, was buried, and rose again. (Jesus also called believers lights of the world. We are the vessels who hold the light. We're supposed to let the light of the good news about Jesus, the gospel, shine through us. Jesus mentioned good works as one way we can let His light shine.)

4. (a) To preach Christ's gospel. (b) Paul's witness seemed to exude a fragrance about knowing Christ.

5. (a) Those being saved and those who were perishing. (b) For those being saved, the gospel was the aroma of life leading to life. For those who were perishing, it was the aroma of death leading to death.

6. So that God gets the credit, not us.

7. Humans have a tendency to take credit for things; God knows this tendency is always lurking in the human heart. He purposely told Gideon that he couldn't use a large army, because Israel would otherwise take the credit, not give it where it belonged—to God.

8. The earthen vessels, our bodies, are hard pressed but not crushed, perplexed but not in despair, persecuted but not forsaken, and struck down but not destroyed.

9. First Corinthians 10:13 assures us that any problem we have is common

to humankind and that God is faithful! He will not allow us to be tempted (tried) beyond what we are able—but will make a way of escape to enable us to bear it.

10. His death and His life. (His death [on the cross] and His life [resurrection] are the essence of the gospel. See 1 Corinthians 15:3 and 4. Our bodies portray both parts of this gospel message.)

11. In dying, we experience the resurrection life of Jesus.

12. Paul's prayer is unusual because he did not want an easy Christian life, but to experience God's power through suffering. He wanted God's righteousness to be evident in him. Furthermore, death was working in his body, but new life was evidenced in the Philippians. As Paul endured suffering and bodily problems while preaching, he knew that some Philippians were being saved and finding new life. This made Paul rejoice.

13. "Labours," stripes above measure, imprisonments, and "deaths" (v. 23); five beatings of thirty-nine lashes each (v. 24); three beatings with rods, one stoning, three shipwrecks (v. 25); many dangers/perils on land and sea, including robbery (v. 26); and extreme exhaustion and exposure to the weather, hunger and thirst, and nakedness (v. 27). (On top of these life-threatening things, Paul had the ordinary, daily bearing of ministry responsibility [v. 28].)

14. (a) Paul called it a thorn in the flesh, a messenger of Satan, lest he be exalted for revelations that he had. (b) Paul had pleaded with the Lord that it might be removed.

15. Instead of taking the problem away, God assured him, "My grace is sufficient for thee." (Some have said that God answers yes, no, or wait. But in this passage we find that God answers yes or "grace"; that is, "My grace is sufficient," instead of answering no or wait.)

16. Paul accepted God's answer and even rejoiced, gladly boasting in his infirmities for Christ's sake, acknowledging that "when I am weak, then am I strong."

17. Christ was crucified in weakness, yet He arose in power, so Paul was content to be weak in Him. Paul knew that he also would live with Jesus by the power of God.

18. Paul was concerned more for the Corinthians than he was for himself. He could accept death or weakness if they resulted in life and strength for the Corinthians. Paul just wanted the Corinthians to be strong and complete in Christ. Their thankfulness would bring glory to God.

19. God wants to make known the riches of His glory in believers. He could do that without us, but He wants to do it through each of us who trust Him as Savior, whom He calls "children" (Romans 9:26).

20. God is like the potter. God, Who owns our "vessels," deserves the privilege of shaping these vessels as He desires, each vessel showing forth His treasure as He deems best. He asks, "Cannot I do with you as this potter [does with the clay]?" And if the clay is marred, He has the power to remake it according to His good pleasure. We can trust the clay pot of our physical bodies to His all-wise goodness, because we belong to Him and He knows what He wants to accomplish through us.

**Weigh In**—(These are personal answers. Some ladies might want to share their responses to question 2, but sharing should be voluntary.)

## LESSON 6

**Warm Up**—1. The psalmist described his circumstances as "the sorrows of death" surrounding him, as "the pains of hell" holding him, and as trouble and sorrow.

2. He believed that God is gracious, righteous, and merciful (v. 5). He also knew that "the LORD preserves the simple" (v. 6). The psalmist must have felt rather simple at that moment.

3. That he prayed because he had faith in God and that he was greatly afflict-ed. (It sounds as if the psalmist felt just as Paul did in 2 Corinthians 4:8 and 9.)

**Work Out**—1. To speak the message of the gospel to the Corinthians, as-suring them of life after death and the power of the gospel to raise them up and make life worth living.

2. That God, Who raised up Jesus' body, would also raise his body.

3. Those who have died in Christ will rise to meet the Lord in the air and live eternally with Him.

4. The same God Who raised Jesus from the dead will raise the dead with Jesus.

5. Paul was thankful to work for the sake of others, because he knew they would also be thankful to God and that this thankfulness would abound and give God the glory (v. 15). He was not discouraged; he said, "We faint not" (v. 16).

6. That a believer's outward man, or physical body, is perishing (or getting old and feeble), but that the "inward man" is renewed day by day.

7. As believers behold the glory of the Lord, the Holy Spirit renews, or transforms, their "inner man" little by little into the image of the Lord, or Christlikeness.

8. Turning away from the influences and opinions of the world and turning instead to meditating on the law of the Lord would renew believers day by day as they heed it. For as they meditate on the Word, the Holy Spirit makes them more like Christ.

9. Both verses talk about renewing our inner man or our minds. Like Psalm 1, Romans 12:2 tells us there is something we should not do: be conformed to the world; and something we should do: be transformed by the renewing of our minds and focusing on the will of the Lord.

10. Paul called the present (time) a "moment" and the future, "eternal." He called the current weight of believers' physical circumstances a "light" affliction; but the future circumstances will have a "far more exceeding" weight, and it will be of glory, not affliction.

11. To things that are not seen, that is, things that are eternal. And we should remember that the things we see—like the affliction in our bodies—are temporary.

12. The purpose of a tent is to provide temporary housing and easy setup and removal; its material will wear out.

13. That when a believer's earthly body house, or tent, dies (the tent is taken down), that believer has an eternal house in Heaven, a building not made with hands.

14. Believers groan because the body is a burden; it is weak and frail. As believers, we long to have bodies that do not die, that is, we long that our "mortality might be swallowed up of life." (This is not a death wish. We don't really want to lose this body, but we yearn for something more permanent; we yearn for immortality, life that will not die. We're not wishing to die so we can have eternal life— but we would like this life rather to be "swallowed up" by immortality.)

15. God has prepared believers for immortality and life, and He has given us His Holy Spirit to guarantee that we actually receive it. The Holy Spirit Who lives in us is our guarantee.

16. Paul said that God "has sealed us and given us the Spirit in our hearts" as a guarantee.

17. Paul said that believers walk by faith and know that if we are absent from the body, we will be present with the Lord. But, admittedly, while we are still at home in our bodies, we are absent from the Lord.

18. Paul's goal was to please the Lord while he was still in this life. Paul kept on this track because he realized that he would face the Judgment Seat of Christ when he left this life, to be rewarded for the things he had done while still in his earthly body, whether good or bad. That is very sobering for believers to remember.

19. We Christians will be judged on the basis of what we have done while we were still in our bodies, whether good or bad.

20. The challenge is to not live for ourselves, but for Jesus, Who died and rose again for us.

**Weigh In**—(Ask for volunteers to share their answers to the Weigh In questions. These are personal, so don't pressure the ladies to share. Their fears and concerns are real and should not be taken lightly. Only the Lord can replace fear with faith or concern with confidence in Him. That is the work of the Holy Spirit, and it comes over a lifetime of living and trusting, as we are "changed into the same image from glory to glory, even as by the Spirit of the Lord" [2 Corinthians 3:18]. This is not the time to be preachy. If some do share their concerns, it might be helpful to have prayer for all, asking the Lord to give each one a growing confidence in God's promises until you all come to think as Paul did.)

## LESSON 7
**Warm Up**—1. Paul used the word picture of a temple to describe the believer.

2. Special features of Solomon's temple were its symmetry (dimensions), color (blue, purple, scarlet), beauty (overlaid with gold, carvings), and design

(the whole plan). It was also holy and filled with God's glory.

3. You are God's temple and He lives in you. The temple should be holy.

**Work Out**—1. Ten times in the King James Version. The count may vary in other versions.

2. The two considerations are (1) Is it expedient or helpful? and (2) Does it have the potential to enslave?

3. These verses teach that a believer is to glorify God in her body, because it is the temple of God and the Spirit dwells in it. The verses also emphasize that our bodies (God's temple) must be holy.

4. *Negative*—The body *is not* for sexual immorality. *Positive*—The body *is* for the Lord and the Lord for the body.

5. God the Father raised Christ's physical body and will raise believers' bodies too.

6. Believers' bodies are important to Christ because they are members of His body of believers.

7. The Holy Spirit makes the believer's body His temple.

8. Two shall be one flesh (Genesis 2:24). Sexual immorality joins not only the believer's body but also God to a harlot because the believer is already joined to God. It sins against the body that all three Persons of the Trinity value and indwell.

9. (a) Fornication (i.e., consensual sexual intercourse between two persons not married to each other) hurts the body. (b) Emphasizing this fact shows the value God places on the body.

10. *Verse 19*—Because you're a believer, your body is God's temple; you are not your own. *Verse 20*—As a believer, you were bought at a price so you could be a temple for the Holy Spirit.

11. (a) Peter said that the believer's body was bought at the high price of Christ's precious blood. (b) This price was not corruptible, like mere silver or gold, which decays. It was the "precious" blood, like that of a spotless lamb. (c) It has a very high, incomparable value.

12. (a) Flee! (Discuss: There are some sins you have to stand up to and fight. Why isn't sexual sin one of them?) (b) You can "flee," or run, by doing things such as turn off television shows, videos, or computers; turn your back at check-out counters; refuse to buy or read certain books or magazines. If you turn away from a pornographic joke or picture, you mentally decide to glorify God in your body. (Ask God for His help. He cares. Remember David, who did not flee; he beheld, he took a long look, and he destroyed his testimony and brought heartache to his family.)

13. When he was tempted, he literally left his cloak and fled. He took dramatic physical action to remain pure.

14. To prevent sexual immorality.

15. "Wife" and "husband," "affection due her," "her own body," "his own body."

16. The word "likewise" conveys mutual responsibility: "Let the husband [do this] *likewise* also the wife [do this]" (v. 3); "the wife does not [do this] *likewise* the husband does not [do this]" (v. 4) (italics added). (Explain: The word "likewise" is used to balance the submission of both husband and wife. Notice how careful Paul was to be fair to both. He not only used the word "likewise" in both verses 3 and 4, but he also started one sentence with the husband and the other with the wife. It's as though—not only with words, but in the very order of his words—Paul was emphasizing that this most intimate of relationships is to be a mutual relationship of satisfying and submitting by both persons.

17. The words "render," "unto," "likewise," and "also" convey that both spouses should gain sexual satisfaction from the marital sexual relationship. The husband should "render" affection due to his wife; "likewise" the wife to her husband. (Illustrate: Think about the "nonsexual hug." Most women like a nonsexual hug—a hug that says I love you without wanting anything from you. This can lead to sexual desire in a woman, though she may not start out with that intent. Her desire to be loved or satisfied may be met by that hug. This may make the husband's job a little more difficult, since it may not be easy for a man to think about satisfying his wife without thinking immediately of sexual fulfillment.) (Note: The married women in your group may want to talk about themselves, but avoid letting them discuss personal information about their husbands.)

18. A wife may sometimes submit to her husband's desire, even though she is tired. On the other hand, a husband may submit to his wife and bring his body under control and not require fulfillment if he senses his wife is worried about the children, for example. This is an area of learning. According to Charlie Shedd, author of *Letters to Karen,* and *Letters to Philip,* "Sex is a twenty-year warm-up." In other words, expect it to be a learning process.)

19. "Consent" implies that a couple have talked about sexual abstinence, and "for a time" implies that abstinence should not last long. (A couple should be able to talk about this area of their life together. That is why several questions have encouraged the women to do just that. Encourage them to keep those intimate conversations between themselves and their husbands alone. Remind them, if necessary, that their personal, marital conversations are not appropriate for discussion at your Bible study.)

20. Two examples of how Satan could use consensual abstinence to tempt a spouse who is feeling deprived are (1) the boss at work compliments his secretary, thereby satisfying a starved need for affirmation and arousing an appetite for sexual satisfaction; (2) the husband works with beautiful women all day and feels starved sexually when he always comes home to a disheveled wife. (Answers will vary.)

**Weigh In**—(Weigh In answers are exceptionally personal in this lesson, so it is wise not to encourage sharing. However, if you feel comfortable doing so, encourage the ladies to talk privately with you, your pastor, or your pastor's wife if they are struggling in the area of sexual purity. Any confidence shared with you must always be kept private—a matter for your personal prayer.)

## LESSON 8
**Warm Up**—1. Individual answers will vary.

|  | My List | Her List |
|---|---|---|
| How much time do you spend shopping? |  | I bring food from afar (v. 14); rise early to provide food (v. 15); shop for wool, flax (v. 13), and land (v. 16), as well as for food. |
| What are your main concerns when you shop for food? |  | I want quality food and will work to get it or to plant it myself. I want to have enough for my household, my household staff, and the poor (vv. 15, 16, 20). |
| What are your concerns when you shop for clothing? |  | I want quality merchandise (v. 18); warm clothes for my family (v. 21); and attractive clothes of tapestry, silk, and purple (v. 22). |

2. Answers will vary. Legitimate needs turn to worry when a woman begins to fear instead of trust God to meet her needs.

3. They worry about eating too much or getting fat from what they eat.

4. (a) Individual answers will vary. (b) (Ask: What is your opinion, and can you think of any Scripture verses to support it?)

5. Individual answers will vary. (Ask: Can you think of any verses to support this statement?)

**Work Out**—1. The treasures of earth can decay, rust, be destroyed, or be stolen.

2. Your treasure drags your heart along with it.

3. The eye is the gate by which attractions on this earth get through to the body. The entire body is affected by the eye, either made completely light or completely dark.

4. (a) A person with an evil eye hastens after riches. (b) Proverbs 23:6 and 7 advise us not to keep close company with a person who has this kind of eye, nor to desire what he has. It is obvious that we are easily influenced by the people we spend time with.

5. To disperse light. (If someone wants to give light to others, it does no good to put a lamp under a basket, but on a lamp stand. Verse 36 adds that a body full of light is like a lamp shining brightly and giving light.)

6. (a) An evil eye, or having an eye that hastens after riches, can make the lamp of the body dark. (b) The body that is supposed to be a light of witness by good works is dark. Seeking after riches apparently hinders our doing the good works that glorify our Father in Heaven.

7. (a) A very rich man decided to build bigger barns to store his stuff, but God

did not allow him to keep his wealth. (b) By storing up treasure on earth, the rich farmer was not rich toward God. He valued possessions, rather than a right relationship to God. (c) This story highlights that it is possible to value the passing riches of this life over a relationship with God and pleasing Him.

8. Jesus warned that you will either love the one (that is, God or "mammon") and hate the other (God or material wealth), or you will be loyal to one (God or material possessions) and despise the other (God or material wealth/possessions). You cannot serve two masters. Obviously, God wants to be master of our riches.

9. (1) Food or drink, (2) clothing, (3) stature. (Discuss: What happens when we allow the cravings of our bodies to go unchecked? Possible answers: Unchecked craving for alcohol turns a person into an alcoholic; an unchecked appetite will lead to obesity.)

10. The body is more than clothing, and life is more than food. (Luke 12:15 adds that life is more than possessions. Our bodies have value beyond the kinds of clothing we wear.)

11. Your Father feeds the birds even though they don't store food in barns, so trust Him to feed you too.

12. Worry about height doesn't work, because it won't change anything.

13. Lilies do not work; they don't "spin" cloth to clothe themselves, while people do both. God clothes the lilies, and Solomon in all his glory could not compare to their beauty. (Perhaps this indicates that God might even care about "style"—as long as it is His concern and not ours.)

14. God even cares about clothing grass; surely He cares about clothing you. (Interesting! How often do you talk to Him about your clothing?)

15. "Seek" and "need."

16. The Gentiles—people in general—all seek food, clothing, and how to improve their stature or figure.

17. The kingdom of God. (God desires that we seek His kingdom and His righteousness and that we trust Him for our needs. When we seek things that are important to Him, He will provide things that are important to us, like our temporal needs.)

18. (a) Believers' Heavenly Father knows our needs even before we ask Him about them. (God knows our bodily needs, and He wants to care for them. Therefore, we can pray about them; we can trust Him to provide for our needs.) (b) Individual answers will vary.

19. Pray about these things with an understanding and true desire to want His will in these matters more than my own. (Discuss: Does God have a will concerning clothing and fashion? Answer: Yes, His will is that we desire His will "be done on earth" in our life situations—not in some ethereal matter way out there, but in our specific needs and situations. Ask Him to help you avoid temptations to desire more than what He wills for you or something different than He wills for you. First Timothy 6:6–11 and 17–19 is a wonderful companion passage! A time-worthy comparison!)

20. Seeking the kingdom of God is akin to godliness. In Paul's mind, it is contentment with the things that God provides along the way—these add up to gain, or real treasure.

21. Paul warned that seeking to be rich can cause a person to fall into temptation and a snare, foolish and hurtful lusts (that drown people in destruction and eternal damnation), all kinds of evil, and many sorrows.

22. Flee these things.

23. *Don't* be haughty because you have money. *Don't* trust in your money. *Do* realize that God is the One Who gave it to you and that He likes to see you enjoy what He has given. *Do* good; be rich in good works. (God gives to you so you can do good things for others.)

24. You store up treasure and a good foundation for the future. (This would be laying hold of eternal life, storing up treasures in Heaven, or living with eternal values in view.)

**Weigh In**—(Give the ladies an opportunity to pray together at the end, specifically praying aloud for their own needs and asking the Lord for wisdom in seeking His kingdom first.)

## LESSON 9

**Warm Up**—(Ask if any of the women kept a record of how she spent her time on her body. Did the ladies learn anything from keeping the list?)

**Work Out**—1. Present them as living sacrifices *to* God.

2. (a) It is reasonable to present our bodies to God. (b) Individual responses. It is reasonable, since God is the creator and ultimate sustainer. He knows how the body is made, with all of its intricacies, and He is the best one to make it function properly. He also knows our future and what is really best for us.

3. Except for the scapegoat, most sacrifices in the Old Testament were dead; their necks were slit and their blood was shed. (In Romans 12:1, God is not asking us to die for Him; He wants us to live for Him.)

4. "Holy" and "acceptable" to God. (Only a holy sacrifice is acceptable to God. Wow! Only He can make us holy! And He wants to.)

5. Paul wanted us believers to avoid the alternative: giving our bodies over to sin. (Sin wants to reign, or rule, in our bodies. Sin wants us to obey its lusts. Sin wants to enslave us. As Satan offered Eve something new and wonderful but then enslaved her, so he still tries to entice us to yield our bodies to sin. Many people fall. Unfortunately, even many believers. God wants us to offer our bodies for righteousness and holiness, not for sin and death. He wants us to be mastered by Him, not by sin. He knows that we will be slaves to whatever or whomever we present our bodies. God wants a holy sacrifice, not a sinful sacrifice.)

**Pulse Check**—(Ask if a volunteer would tell of a past time when she presented her body to the Lord in a dedicatory way. You might also ask if anyone decided to make such a decision this week, and if she would like to tell about it. But don't pressure for an answer. After waiting only a minute or so, you might say a short prayer, perhaps asking the Lord to help all, or rededicating your own body to the Lord. But keep personal things private.)

6. (a) God desires our minds. (b) Giving God our minds results in our not being conformed to the world, but being transformed by the renewing of our minds. (What we think influences what we do. Thinking is the "root"; living is the "fruit.")

7. Good, acceptable, perfect (KJV).

8. Romans 12:2 says, "Be not conformed to this world." That's what Psalm 1:1 also means when it says that the blessed man doesn't stand, sit, or walk in counsel that comes from the ungodly, sinners, and the scornful. We should avoid these.

9. (a) God says we should not think too highly of ourselves, but should think soberly, or seriously. (We shouldn't be comparing ourselves and putting ourselves higher. Unsaved people often take credit for their abilities. They ascribe it to their expertise, or their hard work, and so forth. They often compare themselves with other people.) (b) Romans 12:16 is similar when it says we should not have our minds on high things. (Thinking of high things encourages us to keep comparing, to look for people we think are better, to associate with them, rather than with people we think are lowly. Our society encourages us to rub shoulders with the higher-ups, to use people to gain promotions, and the like.)

10. We should realize that God has given every one of us something special (that is, a spiritual gift), so we shouldn't think less of ourselves. (Verse 6 tells us we have received a gift of grace. Our gifts will differ in some ways. But each one comes from God and His grace, so it must be special, and we should be encouraged by that.)

11. (a) First Corinthians 4:6 and 7 remind us that thinking higher is being puffed up. (b) There is no logical reason for being proud, because it is God Who makes us different, and everything we have, every talent or ability, comes from God. It is a gift; therefore, we cannot boast about it. What the other person has is her gift from God. (Dare we classify her gift or ours as less valuable to God?)

12. Our bodies have many parts: head, eyes, arms, legs, stomach, heart, feet, hands, etc. Each of these body parts has a different job or serves a different function. The word "office" in some versions means "function." In the Body of Christ all believers have different functions too.

13. Paul stated that the Body of Christ is a group of people and members of one another. (It is informative to pay attention to the many times we read the words "one another" in the New Testament. We learn from this how much God cares about our relationships with one another.)

14. First Corinthians 12:20 and 27 repeat the message of Romans 12:5. Verse 20 says we are many members in one body, and verse 27 calls the believers the Body of Christ and members individually.

15. First Peter 4:8–11 basically says that if you have a gift, use it, just as Paul said in Romans 12. Peter also said that using our gifts makes us good stewards, or managers, of God's manifold (diversified and various) grace.

16. and 17. A transformed mind will evidence . . .

| Verse | This Action or Attitude | Not This |
|---|---|---|
| 9 | Show sincere love for someone. | Not dissimulation, hypocrisy, or pretense |
| 9 | Cleave to good (see verse 2); by implication, hate evil. | Not evil |
| 10 | Show kindness and brotherly love to others. | Not hate and unkindness |
| 10 | Prefer, or honor, other people. | Not a "me-first" attitude |
| 10 | Put other people's concerns before ours. | Not selfish |
| 11 | Be diligent, with a positive attitude, fervent in spirit. Serve the Lord. | Not lazy on the job |
| 12 | Be positive, or have a hopeful attitude. | Not negative |
| 12 | Be patient, waiting on others and on the Lord. | Not impatient, especially during trouble |
| 12 | Be prayerful. | Not worrying |
| 13 | Give or share with others when we see needs. | Not selfish |
| 13 | Open our homes and hearts as we have opportunity. | Not discouraging people from entering our homes or our hearts |
| 14 | Bless others. | Not cursing, not losing our temper with people |
| 15 | Rejoice with people at happy occasions. (Ask for examples.) | Not jealous of their successes or new car |
| 15 | Weep with people at sad times. (Ask for examples.) | Not insensitive to people's hurts |
| 16 | Be of the same mind; accept people. | Not comparing people; not thinking we are better or worse than others. |
| 16 | Recognize that all we have is from God. | Not ungrateful |
| 17 | Do what is right. | Not repaying evil with evil |
| 18 | Strive for peace with the saved and the unsaved. | Not argumentative |
| 19 | Let God avenge us and others. | Not vengeful for self, trying to get even |
| 20 | Feed your enemy. | Not hope for evil against that person |
| 21 | Overcome evil with good. | Not overcome by evil or discouraged by it |

**Weigh In**—(Perhaps give opportunity for one or two ladies to share a testimony of the time she dedicated her body to the Lord or came to a new understanding of dedication of one's body. As always, never press for personal sharing.)

## LESSON 10

**Warm Up**—1. Answers might include the following: We get tired and have to sleep; we get hungry and have to eat; we age; we get weary from travel.

2. Jesus never had limitations of any kind before He took on flesh. He was never hungry or tired or weary. He never had to travel from place to place. He never had to feel pain or physical suffering.

**Work Out**—1. Jesus was conceived by the Holy Spirit.

2. God allowed Jesus to have a human mother.

3. He grew in wisdom, spirit, stature or height, and in social graces ("in favor with . . . man"). Perhaps He learned to say "please" and "thank you," similar to the social graces we teach our children.

4. Even though Jesus knew a lot and was learning a lot, as a young person, almost a teen, He obeyed his parents.

5. *John 4:6*—weariness; *John 4:7; 19:28*—thirst; *Matthew 4:2; Mark 11:12*—hunger; *Luke 8:23*—tired, needed to sleep.

6. (a) The similarities were that Satan tempted both Eve and Jesus when they were alone; he attacked the claims of God (to Jesus, "If you are the Son of God . . ."; to Eve, "You will not surely die"); Satan offered what he could not provide (to Eve, the ability to be like God; to Jesus, power and authority that Jesus as God had anyway). (b) Jesus was first tempted to meet His hunger with bread; Eve was tempted with something to eat. (c) Eve yielded to Satan; Jesus did not.

7. Jesus knew exactly what God had said and used Scripture accurately to defend against Satan's lies. We should learn Scripture, too, so we can be ready to answer Satan's lies.

8. Since Jesus was tempted, He can help us when we are tempted. He knows what temptation feels like—though He did not yield.

9. He got alone and prayed, sometimes all night. No wonder Hebrews 4:15, our key verse, urges us to call out to Him in prayer.

10. Jesus became obedient unto death, even the death of the cross. With words of submission or obedience, He said, "Not my will, but thine by done."

11. Jesus was bound by priests and elders (v. 27), was scourged by Pilate's men (v. 26), had a crown of thorns put on his head (v. 29), was spit on (v. 30), was struck with a reed, and was crucified (v. 35). (The Scriptures do not record the horrors of the actual crucifixion. They simply state the fact.)

12. "I come to do thy will, O God."

13. We ought to lay our lives down for other believers as Christ did for us. The least we can do is give up our rights for the sake of another believer.

14. Suffering for doing what is good or right.

15. Christ's suffering is an example for us in our own suffering.

16. When reviled, He did not revile, or give verbal abuse, in return. Neither did

He threaten, but He committed Himself to Him Who judges righteously.

17. If we suffer in the will of God, we should commit our souls to Him in doing good as to a faithful Creator (1 Peter 4:19)—in the same way that Christ committed Himself to God, Who judges righteously (2:23).

18. We should live unto (concerned with) righteousness.

19. *Matthew 26:39*—He prayed and asked for God's will to be done. *Mark 14:36*—He confessed that God had power to change His circumstance, but prayed for God's will instead of His own. *Luke 22:42*—He prayed that God would remove the trial but only if it was His will. *Luke 23:46*—He commended His spirit to God the Father.

**Weigh In**—(If time permits, let ladies share verses they have memorized that help them deal with temptation or suffering.)

## LESSON 11

**Warm Up**—1. Individual answers.

2. Personal answers. For example, a thirty-year-old would have 14,600 days left. A seventy-seven-year-old has enjoyed 2,555 days more than the average.

**Work Out**—1. "The adoption," that is, the redemption of our bodies.

2. (a) "In Christ" we (believers) will be "made alive." (b) The fact that Christ rose from the dead and is the "firstfruits" of those who have died in Christ.

3. (a) Death. (b) Christ will destroy death.

4. How will the dead be raised? What kind of a body will they have?

5. We will have a new and better body. It will be (1) incorruptible (it will not be affected by the ravages of sin; it will not decay, age, or wear out); (2) raised in glory; (3) raised in power; (4) spiritual, rather than natural (that is, it will be empowered by spirit, yet still be physical). (There must be as much difference between corruptible/incorruptible and mortal/immortal as there is between a seed of corn and a full ear of corn.)

6. The flesh and blood we have now are corruptible, subject to decay and death, because of the original sin inherited from our father, Adam. Our corruptible must put on incorruptible, and our mortal must put on immortality. We must have bodies that are not subject to decay or death. This is not possible without God's miraculously changing us.

7. A trumpet will sound from Heaven; the dead will be raised incorruptible; and we who are still alive, or who have not fallen "asleep," will be changed. Our bodies will be changed. We will put on incorruption and immortality—a body that cannot decay. Wow!

8. In a "moment," in a "twinkling of an eye." That's fast.

9. When mortal bodies become immortal, death will be conquered.

10. (a) A trumpet will sound. The dead will rise, and so will those who have not died. (b) God will bring with Him those who have already died, or fallen asleep (v. 14); the bodies of dead believers will be raised from their graves at the same time that God the Son brings them with Him (v. 16); the believers who are alive will not "prevent," or precede, those who have died (vv. 15, 17); believers will

meet the Lord and be with the Lord (v. 17).

11. Verse 13—"asleep"; verse 14—"sleep in Jesus"; verse 15—"asleep"; verse 16—"dead in Christ."

12. Luke said he had "infallible proofs." He summarized them as Jesus had been seen by the apostles on many occasions for a period of forty days after His resurrection.

13. (a) They risked arrest and beatings; they actually were arrested several times. By Acts 12, James, one of the disciples, had been killed. But the other disciples continued to share the gospel despite the risks. (b) *Acts 2:32*—During his first message to the crowd on the Day of Pentecost, Peter claimed that Christ arose. *Acts 3:14–26*—Peter spoke to the crowd that gathered after he healed the lame beggar. Peter frankly told them that they had crucified Jesus but that God had raised Him. He called Jesus the "Prince of life." *Acts 4:18–29*—The disciples were arrested and taken into custody for the night and then ordered not to speak in the name of Jesus. They were threatened, but they continued to speak of their risen Lord and how His life fulfilled Old Testament Scriptures. *Acts 5:29–32*—They were arrested and put into the common prison. Then they were released by an angel and were found preaching again in the temple the very next morning. When the officers came to question them, the disciples told them that "we ought to obey God rather than men" and again affirmed that God had raised Jesus from the dead, the very One Whom they had killed.

14. Peter explained that Psalm 16 affirms that Jesus' body could not decay or remain in the tomb and that this prophecy couldn't refer to David, whose body did decay and remain in the tomb. From Psalm 110, Peter affirmed that David did not ascend into the heavens, so the "my lord" in verse 1 had to be Jesus, Whom God raised.

15. Paul used Psalm 2:7 to show that the day of Jesus' resurrection is the day specifically meant by "this day" in "this day I have begotten you." And on the basis of His resurrection, Jesus has the authority to be an eternal high priest. Paul also used Psalm 16, as Peter did, to show that Jesus could not decay or remain in the grave, even though He had died.

16. When Paul saw a vision of immense light and heard the voice of a glorified Person in the heavens, he asked, "Who art thou, Lord?" and the answer came back, "I am Jesus whom thou persecutest." There was never any debate after that. Paul immediately wanted to know how he could obey the Lord—Whom he preached the rest of his life.

17. He was seen by Cephas, then by all eleven disciples and then by a large group of over five hundred at one time—most of whom were still alive when Paul wrote (so could testify if asked by any of Paul's readers). Then Jesus was seen by James, then all the apostles, and, of course, by Paul at his conversion. (Paul saw Jesus in Heaven, and he was convinced enough to join the Christians rather than continue trying to get rid of them.)

18. Our bodies will be transformed to be conformed to Jesus' glorious body.

19. We will be like Jesus, for we shall see Him as He is.

20. Jesus, God's Son, is heir of all things (1:2), the one through Whom God created the worlds (1:2), the brightness of God's glory (1:3), the express image of God's person (1:3), the One Who upholds all things by the word of His power (1:3), so much better than angels (1:4), sitting on the right hand of God on His throne (8:1).

21. Jesus is clothed in a garment to His feet (v. 13), has a gold band around His chest (1:13), has hair as white as wool or snow (1:14), has eyes like a flame of fire (1:14), has feet like refined brass (1:15), has a voice like many waters (1:15). He has a sword coming from His mouth and holds stars in His hand (1:16). His countenance is as bright as the sun (1:16). (John fell at His feet as if he were dead. If this is the same way that Christ appeared to Paul on the road to Damascus, you can understand why Paul was blinded by such a light.)

22. *Glory*—The glory of Jesus Christ makes Him the Lion of the tribe of Judah. *Humanity*—In His humanity, He is the "Root of David." No wonder it is important for us to know His genealogy.

23. (a) Jesus the Lamb stands in the midst of the throne, the four living creatures, and the twenty-four elders—in the very midst of the throne where God sits. (b) The four living creatures and the elders will fall down in worship, each with a harp and golden bowls of incense, the prayers of the saints. Then they will sing a wonderful new song of worship: "Thou art worthy to take the book and to open the seals thereof: for thou wast slain, and hast redeemed us to God by thy blood out of every kindred and tongue, and people, and nation"! (If there were any leader with this much influence in our day, we would honor him greatly. This is our Savior, Jesus, the only One Who has this kind of power. How can we not honor Him with our lives?)

**Weigh In**—(Give several ladies the opportunity to praise the Lord in prayer for our Resurrection Hope.)